kley   W. Smethurst   Joe Edwards

       18   20

Geo. Geggie   John Lees   H. Geggie

   17   19   21

      7   9   11   13

ire John Stelfox J. W. Bentley J. Clements Wm. Prescott

   6   8   10   12

Simonite Edmund Shaw Thos. Lord T. Helliwell

THE AURICULA

Auricula Tomboy
Auricula Adrian
Auricula Barbarella
Auricula Pippin
Auricula Connaught Court
Auricula Lord Saye and Sele.

Light Centre Alpine 'Dilly Dilly'

THE AURICULA
HISTORY, CULTIVATION AND VARIETIES

Primula auricula

Allan Guest

Garden • Art • Press

British Library Cataloguing-in-Publication Data
A catalogue record for this book is available from the British Library

MIX
Paper from
responsible sources
FSC® C104723

Printed in China
for Garden Art Press, an imprint of ACC Art Books Ltd.

CONTENTS

ACKNOWLEDGEMENTS

I should like to express my thanks to all of those who have made a contribution to the writing of this book. I am deeply indebted to the Midlands and West Section of the National Auricula and Primula Society for allowing me to plunder their archive for a good number of the illustrations and to David Tarver, the Secretary of the Midlands and West Section, for his ready help and support throughout. David, a sculptor by calling, also provided the black and white drawings used to illustrate parts of the text.

My sincere thanks go out to those who came up with the photographs which speak so much more at times than my words. The photographers are:

Les Allen
Ken Bowser
Brian Coop
Scilla Edwards
Lynn Guest, my wife and a constant prop when the words would not come
Keith Leeming
Derek Parsons
Derek Salt
Robert Taylor.

There are also growers such as John Cattle, Brian Clarke, John Gibson, Chris Gill, Terry Mitchell and Roger Woods who are not mentioned in the text but who exhibit plants of the highest quality, the beauty of which I have studied and endeavoured to express. Discussions with them helped in my assessment of plants' merits and failings.

I am particularly indebted to Diana Steel and to her friendly and helpful staff at ACC for having the courage to take on a book which caters for a relatively small group of enthusiasts but which seeks to bring the beauty and serenity of these fascinating yet tantalising flowers to a wider public. I hope that their faith is justified.

Allan Guest

INTRODUCTION AND GLOSSARY

The auricula is a small, herbaceous perennial whose ancestors came from the upper regions of the Alps. It has two main progenitors, probably with other species adding smaller contributions along the way. In winter it dies down to a small resting bud at the top of a tap root, though side stems may offer several of these buds. In spring its leaves emerge from the main stem or stems and elongate. Flowers are carried in groups on top of single stems which spring up from amongst the leaves. Some forms are highly scented; others have lost this attraction.

Although hardy in nature, because the flowers have fascinated people for so long, forms far removed from the natural types have been bred. Aspects of the blooms have appealed to something deep inside human beings almost from the time of their introduction into cultivation. Sometimes it was the sheer novelty of new types, sometimes something much more mysterious, namely a proportion and form which derives from the apparently instinctive feeling in the European mind that certain measures and shapes represent an aspect of our universe which is difficult to explain. All of this is discussed later in this book.

The cultivators of the auricula have come mainly from western Europe and from all levels of society. However, since so many of those who have made a contribution to its development have been working men with no great education, some of the terminology applied in describing the plants and used throughout this book comes from their world. Other expressions are a matter of common sense. Occasionally proper botanical terms are employed. All of these are listed in the glossary which follows. I hope that the more erudite reader will pardon my explanations of such terms and that the old hands will not find my explanations of their familiar vocabulary too trite.

anther	the small sack at the end of a stamen which contains pollen
body colour	the coloured ring between the paste and the innermost part of the edge on an Edged Auricula
calyx	the cup of small leaf-like structures from which the individual blooms unfold (Latin for a goblet or chalice)
carrot	the main root stem or tap root, so called because of its shape
china edge	a thin line of meal which may run round the very edge of the petals of an Edged Auricula
cockled	a wavy formation which occurs where two adjacent petals collide and their edges rise, since neither will slide gracefully under its neighbour; named from its resemblance to the sea shell
collar	the section of the main root stem or carrot which lies at soil level
corolla	the face or disc of an individual bloom
crenation	small notches running round the rim of the central tube

farina	the white powder on the flowers and leaves of many primulas; the Latin word for 'flour', it is also known as 'meal'
ground	another word for 'body colour'
Long Tom	a plant pot with a longer main body than is usual
meal	another word for 'farina'
paste	the brilliant ring of white farina between the tube and the body colour of Show and Striped Auriculas
pedicel	the footstalk of an individual bloom which connects the bloom to the scape
petaloid	becoming like a petal
pin-eye(d)	when the stigma and the style in the centre of the tube rise above the anthers. The shape of this organ resembles a pin. Pin-eyed plants may not be shown except in classes for Border Auriculas.
pip	an individual bloom
scape	the stem which rises from amongst the leaves and carries the head of flowers
stamen	the whole male unit of the reproductive parts of a flower
stigma	the tip of the female reproductive parts to which pollen is applied in hybridisation
style	the female reproductive parts of a pip in the centre of the tube
thrum-eye(d)	when the stamens and their anthers lie at the top of the central tube of a pip (a thrum is a small fringe of unwoven threads on a loom)
truss	a head of pips
tube	situated at the centre of a bloom and containing the reproductive organs

The Anatomy of an Auricula

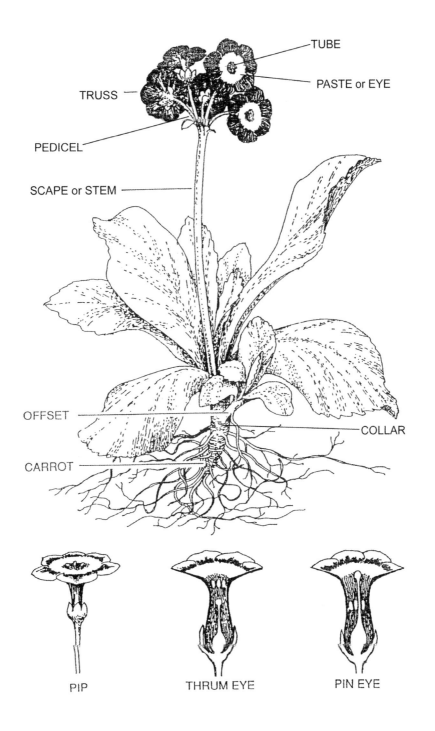

TUBE

PASTE or EYE

TRUSS

PEDICEL

SCAPE or STEM

OFFSET

COLLAR

CARROT

PIP

THRUM EYE

PIN EYE

Chapter 1
HISTORY AND DEVELOPMENT

The auricula has captivated the minds of the majority of people who see it in bloom since it was first brought down from the Alps. Even by the time of its first descent to the flatland it had undergone several changes and had been taken up by a variety of people. The journey made by the members of the species, the combination and re-combination of their characteristics, the men and women who have tended the plants and the social and political circumstances which have surrounded them have all formed an engrossing story. The sight, the scent and the amazing form of auricula blooms bring many an innocent, present-day viewer to a standstill when they first encounter the plants at a garden centre, on a market stall, in a garden border or on a showbench. The colours range from white and yellow via mauve and purple to pink, red, orange, brown and something close to black. The only colour missing from the list is the true blue of the forget-me-not tribe, though there are blooms which most gardeners would describe as blue, just as they would the aubrieta and the campanula. The flowers may be the single, five-petalled disc of the wild species; they may bear several more petals or they may be fully double, with numerous layers of petals. But in the midst of that range is a group of flowers which has undergone a transformation that occurs in very few flower families and none has increased in its beauty as much as the auricula. So where did it all start?

EARLY HISTORY
The early history of the auricula is vague. The plant was not called by the same name by those who first cultivated it and some of the earliest names now apply to totally different species. It is only when descriptions are given that we can be reasonably sure that they were talking about auriculas. Its modern name, *Primula auricula,* stems from the system of naming invented by the Swedish biologist, Carl Linnaeus. Our word, auricula, is the Latinised form of the name given to it in the Alps from which it came. The shape of the leaf was thought to resemble a small bear's ear and this was therefore put into Latin as 'auricula ursi'.

Like most plants, it was believed to have some medicinal properties. The apothecaries held that various parts of the plant were a defence against many complaints varying from colds in the head to vertigo. Fortunately, its bright colour and its scent had recommended

A wild *Primula auricula*, one of two wild parents of our modern plants.

Primula hirsuta, formerly known as *Primula rubra*, the other parent.

the flower to ordinary men and women who cultivated it purely for their own pleasure. We believe, for example, that auriculas were grown in Nuremberg in the late 1400s. The plants must, therefore, have been deemed worthy of being transported there from the mountainous parts of Bavaria, Austria and Switzerland. *Primula auricula* is a small perennial plant with a long root, persistent leaves of a leathery nature that carry a powdery, white coating, and yellow flowers carried in a small head at the top of a single stem. When we come to the first documents which mention the 'bear's ear', a problem appears to arise.

An illustration of the species form of *Primula auricula* was made by the Swiss Conrad Gessner and dates back to before 1565. A number of plants were then described in two works of

1583 and 1601 by the Imperial Court Botanist in Vienna, Charles de l'Ecluse, whose name was translated into Latin as Clusius. He had seen them in various places with blooms in colours other than the wild yellow, some with plain leaves and some with powdered leaves. He regarded each form as a distinct type of plant. We know that Clusius had attempted to cultivate other Alpine plants without success, but whether this also applied to coloured auriculas is uncertain. He did, however, search for them in the Alps and found none. Then, while he was staying in Vienna, the history of the auricula took a new turn. He was enjoying the hospitality of his old friend, Professor Johannes Aichholtz, who was the proud owner of two apparently different types of auricula. One, the wild, yellow-flowered type with mealy leaves, Clusius called 'Auricula ursi I'. The other was in a shade influenced by red and was just the sort of plant he had been seeking; this latter he called 'Auricula ursi II'. The origin of the second plant was less than exact. Aichholtz had been given it by a lady of some means who in turn said that it grew wild in the vicinity of her summer residence. This was the type of plant which was to be the start of our present-day auricula. Clusius received plants of these two treasures from Aichholtz, persuaded them to thrive and, in his turn, distributed them to his fellow scholars across Europe. This was the beginning of the auricula's recorded history.

It took another three hundred years for more light to be shed on the riddle. By the second half of the nineteenth century Auricula ursi II plants had become known as *Primula pubescens*. In the mid-1800s the Austrian botanist, Anton Kerner von Marilaun, retraced the steps of Clusius and found the spot where Auricula ursi II might well have originated. He discovered an area where the yellow *P. auricula* with its liking for limey soils grew adjacent to *P. hirsuta* which prefers more acid ground. The two had cross-fertilised and produced hybrids of many colours. Not only that, the offspring were robust and capable of producing further progeny. They also carried two sets of characteristics. One parent, *P. auricula*, has mealy leaves, coated in a waxy powder called 'farina' (the Latin word for flour) and carries blooms which consist of yellow tissue with no overlying colouring. The other, *P. hirsuta*, has plain green leaves and its flowers are made up of white basic tissue overlaid with a substance called hirsutin (a type of anthocyanin similar to the medium which colours the beetroot, according to Professor Sir Rowland Biffen, an eminent botanist and twentieth century grower of the auricula) which may colour the flower either red or blue according to the acidity of the underlying cells. Here many will recall the tests for acidity which as children we met in school science lessons. In the hybrids

the foliage could be either green or mealed, while the basic flower tissue could be in any shade from white to yellow. When the anthocyanin from the *P. hirsuta* parentage was superimposed on this tissue, the colour of the blooms ranged from the palest pink and mauve via lavender and brown to the deepest reds and blues verging on black. The hybrids possessed further advantages over many of the favourite flowers of the sixteenth and seventeenth centuries such as the rose, the tulip and the pink or carnation. They were easy to propagate, generally undemanding in their culture and they gave seed which could produce a wide range of novelties in a short time. Kerner von Marilaun had untied an old knot, but the auricula had made its way into the hearts (and pockets) of many others in the meantime.

Tradition has it that the auricula arrived in Britain with the Flemish weavers fleeing religious persecution from around 1570 onwards, but there is no printed evidence for this. The first record we have of the flowers is John Gerard's *Herball* of 1597 in which he lists five varieties. Similarly, Conrad Sweert, a Dutch florist who had a business opposite the Town Hall in Frankfurt am Main in Germany, offered six varieties for sale in his catalogue in 1610. By 1629 Parkinson records twenty 'beare's ears' in his *Paradisi in sole Paradisus terrestris*. Two years after that, in 1631, the first 'Florists' Feast' is recorded in the city of Norwich. A florist at that time was not one who sold flowers for a living; it meant anyone who was interested in the cultivation of flowers. They would meet for a meal and other refreshments, bringing along their blooms for display and competition. Norwich was one of the centres where the Flemish immigrants had settled, although Ruth Duthie, in her excellent little book on Florists' Flowers and Societies, points out that there was no history of florists' societies in Flanders. Nevertheless, the interest in florists' flowers such as the tulip and the auricula grew and the occurrence of the feasts became more frequent and widespread from this time until the industrialisation of Britain. The speculation continues in another splendid book, *Die Aurikel – Geschichte und Kultur einer alten Gartenpflanze,* where the author, Brigitte Wachsmuth, reminds us that the auricula also became a favourite in northern France and wonders whether the religious persecution in the Low Countries had forced other weavers southwards into that area, again taking their plants with them.

In 1640 the French painter, Jacques Linard, was depicting auriculas of various colours including a double. Just eight years on and Jacob Bobart the Elder, who was the keeper of Oxford University Botanic Garden, listed a similarly wide range. His son, also called Jacob Bobart, followed in the post of keeper of the garden and compiled a herbarium (a collection of dried plants) for his 'Hortus Siccus' or 'Dry Garden'. Amongst them are auriculas which include a Double and a number of Stripes. *The Garden Book,* written in 1659 by Sir Thomas Hanmer, a well-travelled gentleman who settled on the border of Shropshire and Powys, included an ever-widening colour range such as 'whites, yellows of all sorts, haire colours, orenges, cherry colours, crimson and other reds, violets, purples, murreys, tawneys, olives, cinnamon colours, ash colours, dunns and what nots'. Furthermore he speaks of two striped auriculas, one purple and white, the other purple and yellow. This remarkable work lay unpublished until 1933. The auricula had made steady progress in Britain in sixty years.

Also in 1659, across the North Sea on the border of Denmark and Germany, Duke Friedrich of Schleswig-Holstein-Gottorf had his flower collection painted. Again, amongst the auriculas depicted are Doubles and Stripes. Present-day breeders can only marvel at the fact that in fifty years the auricula had moved on from a handful of simple garden plants to such a variety of form and colour, for the Doubles and Stripes were practically to disappear in the nineteenth century. It took

chance, persistence, much hard work and time to resurrect these forms from the genes still available to later florists. For the next hundred years, members of the nobility, the landed gentry, the clergy and the medical profession in the German states (for there was no single country called Germany) continued to cultivate the auricula and to publish illustrations of them. These too include the Stripes with multifarious colouring and Doubles. One of the writers, reported in Brigitte Wachsmuth's book, tells of the dangers of praising auriculas offered by Dutch growers, for their price rose the following season.

Fortunately, however, the generous spirit which characterises so many of today's breeders was also evident in mid-seventeenth century Britain. John Rea, a Shropshire plantsman, acknowledged the magnanimity of Sir Thomas Hanmer in providing him with new varieties. Rea's son-in-law, Rev. Samuel Gilbert, was another lover of fine plants. In his *Florist's Vade Mecum* of 1682 he makes mention of two rare Striped Double Auriculas which were traded for enormous sums ranging from four or five pounds up to twenty pounds, a small fortune at that time. This form of auricula disappeared so completely that Rowland Biffen, writing in 1949 in his unsurpassed monograph, *The Auricula,* admitted that 'the gaily striped Doubles of one's fancy are still only in cultivation in the land of one's dreams'. At the time he was of course correct, despite himself raising some plants carrying single striped flowers; but again, fifty years later, breeders such as Ken Whorton and Derek Salt began to produce them by dint of much effort, terrific optimism and a deep insight into the auricula. More of this later, but for now let us continue and see how the auricula fared in the turmoil of the eighteenth century.

In the first hundred or so years of its documented life in Britain, the auricula had seen the end of the expansive Elizabethan age, the coming and going of the more flamboyant of the Stuarts, Cromwell's restrained Commonwealth, the crowning of a Dutch Prince (the monarchy of William and Mary) and, after the death of Queen Anne and the end of the Stuart line, the coronation of the first Hanoverian King of England. The revocation of religious freedom in the western part of Europe, combined with the accession of William of Orange to the English throne, must have encouraged more immigrants from the Low Countries to bring not only their beliefs but also their skills and their flowers to England. After so much political and religious strife, the country was in need of a settled period. Only when stability and peace prevail can the gardener and the florist pursue their interests uninterrupted. This is what appears to have happened.

THE EIGHTEENTH CENTURY

From the early 1700s the auricula settled into a new stage of development in England. Much of Europe was about to enter a period of discontent, war and revolution, but Britain saw new stately mansions built and the landscape considered as a necessary part of its grace. Reynolds, Gainsborough and Constable were to bring colour to their walls and Newton, having published his mathematical work containing his new system, calculus, was just publishing his work *Opticks* and looking at the wonderful colours of light. Handel was working away on music to entertain the new kings and stretch the musical mind. While political power in most of Europe rested with the aristocracy, Parliament held the upper hand in Britain. Its members were the landowners and the merchants for whom production, business and trade were the prime concern. Into this fresh order came a new, exciting type of auricula.

Already the florists of Liège in Flanders ('Luik' as it is called in Flemish) had developed bright colours which exploited the dual make-up of the auricula. Their blooms often had a bright, round, circular eye of white, cream or yellow surrounding the tube at the centre.

Adjacent to the eye was a ring of dark colour. This dark colour shaded to a paler version at the edge of the pip (as the individual flower was called). With a white or pale eye, the pip might shade from dark to light blue, from purple to pink or from wine to mauve. If the eye was golden, the colour ran from crimson to light red or from red-black to brown, orange or peach. In either case the varieties of colour could be endless. The illustrations of these plants are reminiscent of today's Exhibition Alpine Auriculas. Many of the artists who painted flowers were also from Flanders and Holland. Their patrons were obviously wealthy enough to afford the services of a professional painter. Engravings, such as Robert Furber's calendar pieces of 1730, exist from both Britain and Germany but they lack the flamboyance and sometimes the refinement of those painted in oils. The Low Countries had produced a flower to set against their beloved tulip, but it was now that the auricula in England set off on a different, startling trip. A remarkable transformation was under way.

The most popular form at the beginning of the 1700s was the Striped Auricula. The striping appears to have been broken colouring but illustrations from the period show a ring of meal at the centre of some pips. Other paintings also show a scattering of meal on the face of the pips or even as a form of striping. Present-day breeders of Alpine Auriculas have eliminated farina from the new seedlings which they exhibit but it was not uncommon in the 1970s and '80s to come across older varieties which carried specks of farina on the eye. Plants have also appeared in the recent breeding lines of both Striped and Double Auriculas with an even sprinkling of fine farina across their coloured surfaces. Farina was of course originally a property of the foliage of the wild *Primula auricula*. At some point then, in the first half of the eighteenth century, leaf tissue began to appear in the pips. This was not the wholesale replacement of the flower petals by miniature leaves as had happened with the

Green China Rose or even the green version of the common primrose. Instead flecks appeared where stripes of colour were generally found on the face of the pips of some striped varieties and also at the tips of petals. What was more surprising was that flower colour was retained in a band between the tips of the petals and the eye. This ring of colour was further enhanced because the circular centre (eye) of the pip assumed a dense coating of the purest white meal, reminiscent of that found at the centre of the bloom and at the base of the calyx of the wild *Primula auricula*. The florists therefore had a circular bloom with a round, often yellow tube at its heart, a startling white eye, and then either a dark body with white mealy stripes and possibly some yellow flecks or alternatively a dark band round the eye with a ring of petal tips of green, grey or white. Since the outer tip was composed of leaf tissue, it could be plain green, green lightly dusted with meal, giving a grey look, or thickly coated with farina, leading to a gleaming white periphery. The brilliance of these pips seized the eye of the growers and the new type, once firmly established in Britain, spread across Europe under the name of the 'English Auricula'. The Stripes and the Doubles declined in popularity and the new Edged group took on an ascendancy which was to last for two centuries.

We have no record of this evolution from Striped to Edged before the mention of two varieties in nurserymen's lists in the middle of the century. Since it takes time to build up sufficient stock to offer plants for sale, the change must have occurred several years previously. There is also some debate as to precisely how the edge developed and what happened to the stripes. We cannot be certain. The old argument was that the two changes were separate phenomena. Anyone who has bred Striped Auriculas in the last thirty years might disagree. It is not uncommon for the stripes to radiate from the centre, up the edge of the petal and then coalesce around the outer rim. This leaves the individual petal looking rather like a small window with a darker area of colour peeping out from its mealy frame. The body colour of the petal frequently carries a dusting of meal too. In other words, the plant is more like a crude Edged Show Auricula than a Stripe. The goal of the eighteenth century florists was to breed a circle of colour (the body colour or ground) surrounding the white eye (the paste) which was free from specks of farina. Conversely, the present-day breeders of Stripes attempt to produce plants in which no broad, solid ring of green leaf tissue or meal runs round the rim. But at a time when the craftsmen who were growing and breeding the auricula were largely uneducated, no records were left.

We also know that there were auriculas known as 'Painted Ladies' which appear in some of the paintings of the time. They had a central paste and various markings of meal or colour which might be edging, lacing or radial streaks. Here one can only speculate, for breeders of Stripes and Edged plants today know that amongst their seedlings they will find odd flowers with a couple of other variations. In one of these a stripe of colour flashes up the edges of the petals while what should be individual stripes merge to form a block of meal touching the paste and extending to the periphery of the pip. Plants of this type are nowadays deposited on the compost heap when one is breeding Grey or White Edges. The other case occurs only, to my knowledge, in the breeding of Stripes. The face of the pip is evenly sprinkled with farina, looking for all the world like a pink or red cake sprinkled with icing sugar, as in Derek Parsons' 'Hot Lips'. One is left to wonder whether dusted flowers of this type, marked by mealy stripes and further enhanced by a mealy lacing around each petal, are how the Painted Ladies got their name. Certainly, illustrations by the German artist, Johann Weißmantel, from 1785 and reproduced in Brigitte Wachsmuth's book, would point towards this hypothesis.

Suffice it to say that John Slater, in his *Amateur Florist's Guide* of 1862, mentions a

Green Edge called 'Rule Arbiter' and a Grey Edge called 'Hortaine' as having been available in 1757. Isaac Emmerton, writing in the first quarter of the nineteenth century, mentions 'Vice's Green Seedling' as the first Green Edge at about the same time as 'Rule Arbiter'. We have no pictures to show us how these flowers might have looked but for many years this date was considered the starting point for the Edged Show Auricula.

The tradition was delivered a sharp jolt in 1987 when a portrait of a little girl called Martha Rodes was displayed by Sotheby's in London. Young Martha stands next to a large terracotta pot containing a splendid plant of a grey-edged auricula which also presents its face to us. In her right hand she holds a truss of the same type but showing its reverse side. Presumably Martha's family wished to show that they knew something about a good auricula. The portrait is signed C. Steele and is dated 1750. It is perplexing that we have no documentary reference to a Grey Edge at that time but, if the artist was honest in his depiction, this was an edged and not a striped plant. It could be then that the disappearance of the farina from a plant such as that held by the young lady to leave a variation with a bright green edge was what set the new types apart from the older ones. What we do know is that the enthusiasts now began to think about what it was that made their plants beautiful. We also know that the auricula was becoming accessible to less well-off members of society.

One of the advantages of the auricula tribe over competitors in the ranks of the other florists' flowers at the time was that it was quicker and easier to propagate than most. Auriculas were also capable of producing seeds in good quantity and from this seed new varieties readily emerged. The nurserymen were thus able to build up stocks of plants without the delays necessitated by waiting for a tiny bulb of a tulip, for example, to build up to flowering size. This new availability allowed their purchase by those a little less wealthy than

the majority of enthusiasts up to this time. Nor would it be surprising if the odd offset from the plant in the gardens of the prosperous found its way to a less luxurious home via a gardener's pocket. Certainly, any working man who was fortunate enough to show or breed a prize variety would be able to hope for some reward to eke out his wage. The auricula had begun to trickle down through the layers of a stratified society. The economic conditions of the late eighteenth and early nineteenth centuries might not have been easy, but at least Britain was spared the pain of warfare at home, something to be borne in mind at the time when the French Revolution, the social unrest it engendered and the Napoleonic wars were creating havoc across the rest of Europe.

PROBLEMS OF CULTIVATION

We must also consider the problems which the growers faced in their cultivation. Glass was an expensive commodity so that its use as a protection against the elements could not be considered by the majority. Potting composts were a black art. Some of those advocated by leading growers contained items such as sugar baker's scum, goose dung and night soil which would horrify modern florists. True, they left their mixtures to weather for two years, turning them constantly, but they still send a shudder down the spine of twenty-first century growers who have easy access to good, simple, loam-based composts.

Protection from the weather brought its problems then as now. The affluent could afford auricula theatres (see page 149), wooden structures that shut out the worst of the weather from above and on three sides but left the fourth side open with cover provided only in the event of rain which might damage the trusses. Tiered shelves were set up to display the plants and to allow each one of them a good amount of light, while some form of cover was kept to hand in order to preserve the blooms from wind and rain from the front. Those with less cash at their disposal were advised to keep their plants

One of the author's current batch of seedlings, this gives some impression of what the original 'Painted Ladies' of the eighteenth century might have looked like.

in a frame or pit with a cloth cover for overhead protection. Any craftsmen working at home enjoyed an advantage for their plants were close at hand throughout the working day. The weavers, traditionally connected with the auricula, would be particularly favoured here, for their cottages, still to be seen today in many Pennine towns, are blessed with windows running across a whole room. These would permit a good number of plants to be grown in splendid light across the sills.

THE NINETEENTH CENTURY

The German painter, F.A. Kannegießer, working in the period 1800-1807, left some wonderful illustrations of the plants then available. They were divided into two sections, English Auriculas, which were Edged varieties, and Luiker Auriculas or what we would now think of as Alpine Auriculas. But the period after the Napoleonic wars in Germany saw much unrest and the auricula declined in popularity, though Doubles were still being bred there into the 1860s.

Meanwhile, in Britain, the number of auricula varieties obtainable from nurserymen was increasing steadily and the growers were formulating in print their views on what exactly constituted a good auricula. In 1792, James Maddock, a Lancastrian nurseryman who had moved to London, set out his views on the relative proportions of a good auricula

Maddock 1792
1:3:6

Glenny 1832
1:2:4

pip. His ideal would have the tube occupy one-sixth of the corolla; the paste should then extend to halfway across the diameter with the body colour and edge occupying the remaining half. The body colour and the edge should be about the same width. This gave a ratio of 1:3:6 for the pip's constituent parts. The features were to be circular and concentric.

In 1832, George Glenny, another nurseryman of firm and forthright opinion, was inclined to differ. He preferred the tube to be a little broader. His recommendation was that the tube should take up a quarter of the diameter, the paste extend up to a half with the body colour and edge taking up the remainder, thus giving a ratio of 1:2:4.

No firm conclusion has ever been arrived at as to which of the two forms is more attractive to the eyes of the majority. Opinions have varied from one period to the next and even sometimes on a geographical basis. Any plant approximating to either set of proportions or somewhere in between is accepted on the showbench, the main consideration being that the tube should not become too broad. It is noticeable that modern Green Edges tend towards the Glenny 1:2:4 proportions, while many Greys favour the Maddock 1:3:6 scheme. As with so much else in the world of auriculas, these are generalisations and there are always exceptions. For our generation, the

views of the majority of growers and breeders will continue to constitute what is considered most desirable. What the florists of the Maddock and Glenny periods all accepted was that the tube should be golden and round, the pip must be thrum-eyed with bold anthers covering the tube, the paste must be smooth and white, the body colour must be an attractive, uniform shade and the whole pip and its constituent parts must be circular. These stipulations have gone unchanged for two hundred years.

From 1820 onwards the number of flower shows began to multiply with an increasing number of horticultural journals reporting on them. 'An Account of Flowers Shews held in Lancashire, Cheshire and Yorkshire etc.' lists fifty shows for the Auricula and Gold-Laced Polyanthus for the year 1826. Although shows for other florists' flowers were taking place right across Britain, there would seem to be a move north in the cultivation of the auricula. If the landlord of an inn knew his area well enough, he would be able to put up attractive prizes and be confident of drawing in sufficient consumers of food and ale to cover his costs on show day and provide a measure of profit. Some of the prizes offered at shows of this type were monetary but others had a different significance for the participants. A silver spoon or a copper kettle – the latter becoming quite a tradition at the shows, with one still being offered at the South-West show of the National Auricula and Primula Society (Midlands and West Section) – would enable a family to dispense with a similar utensil made of wood or a coarser metal.

Participants at these shows might transport their plants formidable distances over poor roads. Emmerton had recommended in 1819 that any small, horse-drawn vehicle should travel at about eight miles per hour. The less affluent competitors would construct wooden boxes containing a shelf. A round hole was cut into this shelf, just wide enough to hold firmly the collar of an auricula pot, while the height of the box would be sufficient to accommodate the flowering stem and truss. The solid sides, roof and base would shelter the plant from the wind and rain. One of these boxes would be suspended at either end of a yoke borne across the florist's shoulders and, carrying this weight, he would walk, it is said, up to fifteen miles. Even today, with all the convenience of modern motor cars, one still sees odd boxes of this type, usually with two shelves, thus doubling the number of plants which can be transported. If we bear in mind that the florists of that time grew their plants in soil and in terracotta pots much larger than is customary today, we can only admire their dedication and stamina.

In the middle of the nineteenth century there were significant changes both for the auricula and in British society. The deployment of large, steam-powered machines was drawing more people into the towns. The handloom weaver could not hope to compete with mechanical looms of the new wool and cotton mills and many were attracted towards the new centres of work. Coal was needed to fire the steam engines and the increasing number of foundries which led to a demand for more miners. The new agricultural machines reduced the number of farm labourers. On moving to the towns, the rural florists would be hard pressed to find housing with sufficient garden to accommodate their auriculas. Where a house had even the smallest patch of ground, vegetables and the odd pig or chicken would be of greater importance to a family. It is not surprising, therefore, to find that the interest in floriculture and the number of flower shows suffered. We can only wonder at the tenacity of those who thought that the beauty of the auricula was worth some effort and sacrifice.

The flowers themselves were assisted at this point by a number of enthusiasts who took up the cause of the Alpine Auricula. This branch of the family had continued very much as the poor relative of the Edged varieties since the days of the Luiker plants one hundred or more years earlier. One of the chief proponents was Charles Turner, a nurseryman of Slough usually known for the introduction of the Cox's Orange Pippin apple. He began to breed new varieties with striking colours and greater circularity. Others were enthused by the new types and took up the challenge of furthering the improvement. They were aided by the fact that the Alpines will generally set seed more freely than Edged and Self types and have no farina to be spoilt by inclement weather. They are often more vigorous and longer-lived than the Show types, though there are some exceptions.

The middle of the nineteenth century saw the rise of the black body colour in the Edged flowers. No one can give a definite reason for this, though several plausible suggestions have been made. The simplest is that, after the death of Prince Albert in 1861, Queen Victoria took to wearing black and fashion followed the royal example. The auricula, it is said, was no exception. A more likely suggestion lies in the other colours that occur in the Edged varieties. Where there is no colouring, the underlying yellow tissue of *Primula auricula* shows through. It is rare that this occupies a nice, even half of the area outside the paste. It is usually either very broad or very thin, so narrow in fact that it can disappear altogether, leaving a pip with a golden tube, white paste and just a green edge. Pale colours may appear as the ground, making an insignificant contrast with the paste and edge. Reds tend to feather out into a yellow area before the edge. Some of the dark mauve or brown colours are very dowdy. Blue is often accompanied by a pale and insignificant tube. All of the colours tend to shade out from dark to light. Black has the advantage of being both striking and solid. Since the convention then, as now, was that the ground should be a striking, solid colour, there can be little wonder that the black body won the day.

One innovation of the machine age that offered assistance to the florists of Victorian Britain was that the railways began to open up the possibility of travel to a wider section of society. If the small, local shows had decreased, it was still possible for the remaining devotees to meet and show their plants at larger gatherings. We are fortunate too that the auricula continued to find favour with those such as the merchants and industrialists who could afford to employ professional gardeners. They sometimes had considerable collections of several florists' flowers such as tulips, pansies, pinks and carnations in addition to their auriculas and Gold-Laced Polyanthus. Four national auricula exhibitions were held at a variety of venues in the 1860s but an attempt to set up a national society foundered. It was left to one of the great florists, Rev. F.D. Horner, to set things in motion again with the establishment in Manchester of the National Auricula Society which held its first show in 1873. A Southern Section was instituted in 1876 but it took a further twenty-four years for a Midlands Section to follow. The three sections persist to this day. They function autonomously but their ideals remain the same and they are always in communication with each other. Many of today's florists are members of more than one section.

THE TWENTIETH CENTURY

There was obviously a certain camaraderie amongst the founder members, even though some of them look quite fearsome in a photograph taken in 1896 and published in the 1922 Jubilee Report. The Reverend Horner lived up to his Christian ideals by befriending florists from all levels of the stratified Victorian society, even to the extent of travelling to be at the side of a weaver florist who lay dying. Sam Barlow, a mill owner from Rochdale, is said to have had good loam transported to his mill from which any florist amongst his workers was allowed to take a small portion. But not all the founders of the Society came from such well-to-do backgrounds. Ben Simonite, a prodigious raiser of new Edged and Self Show Auriculas, was a cutler from Sheffield. One of his Green Edges named after the writer and fellow florist, Shirley Hibberd, still clings on to existence today. The Alpines continued to be seen by some as slightly lower in standing than the Edged and Self types, an attitude still encountered today but, thankfully, less so, as the varieties now available are so superior to many of their predecessors.

But the Society was seeking to continue a tradition which, like many others, was now coming under attack from those of different persuasions. Increasing industrialisation had led to greater urbanisation but a move away from formality in the sphere of gardening, spearheaded by William Robinson and Gertrude Jekyll, also gained impetus. New plants sent by plant hunters from all around the world continued to find their way to Britain. Hybrids amongst old and new plants were developed systematically, leading to the production of such types as the Hybrid Tea rose. Away from the sphere of horticulture and floriculture, musicians and painters such as Schoenberg and Picasso were producing work which veered sharply away from the existing forms. Jazz and new popular forms of music found new followers with the advent of the gramophone and then of the radio. Football and the new Rugby League became affordable ways of spending Saturday afternoons. Above all, a World War took away a large proportion of the British male population and women still found practically no role in the world of the florists at the time. In 1922 membership of the National Auricula Society's Northern Section stood at fifty-eight with subscriptions ranging from three guineas to five shillings. There was one female member on the roll. Horticulture persisted but the tradition of floriculture diminished.

Fortunately, a small band of enthusiasts maintained the auricula through this decade and the next. Even the hardships of the Second World War and the lean years of the later 1940s could not quite destroy all enthusiasm. The House of Douglas, nurserymen of Great Bookham in Surrey, continued to breed and sell new varieties. Hew Dalrymple and later Cyril Haysom of Bartley Nurseries in Hampshire made their contribution. With so little emanating from commercial sources, however, the private enthusiasts of necessity now began to breed new stock. Fred Buckley of Macclesfield deployed (it is believed) the pollen of quite old varieties of Edged Auriculas to produce new, exciting Green Edges, one of which, 'Chloë', still wins top awards on the showbenches of today and stands as an exemplar for its type. The Buckley plants became more widely available to growers after his death, when the whole collection was purchased by Dr. Duncan Duthie who then began to distribute them. In the 1960s, Dr. Robert Newton, a Manchester surgeon, bred leading auriculas of all types. His Green Edge, 'Roberto', regarded by some growers with a measure of suspicion since it was the child of a cross between a Green Edge and a Grey Edge, continues to take top honours at present-day shows and is featuring in the parentage of new varieties. In the following decade, Derek Telford, an engineer from Huddersfield, began by breeding new Dark and Blue Selfs ('Oakes Blue' hardly ever misses a year on the benches) and then bred an astonishing string of Alpines, too numerous to mention. David Hadfield, the stalwart Secretary of the Northern Section for twenty-five years, gave the growers new varieties of Show Auricula such as 'Figaro',

'Prague', 'Jupiter' and 'Sappho' amongst the Greens, 'Grey Hawk' amongst the Greys and 'Brompton' and 'Moonglow' amongst the Selfs. Peter Ward, the Secretary of the Midlands Section, emulated David Hadfield's achievement with Greys and Whites such as 'Warwick', 'Gavin Ward', 'Brookfield' and 'Sharmans Cross', the difficult Yellow Self, 'Tracy Ward', and several Reds such as 'Cheyenne' and 'Geronimo'.

From 1980 onwards, thanks to the many generations of seedlings from breeders such as Tim Coop, body colours other than black have begun to appear in greater quantity and with constantly improving form. Tim's son, Brian, starting from an ideal of a sky blue Self Auricula, has raised an ever-widening range of colours encompassing pale blue, pink, dove-grey and brown with good substance of petal to add their beauty to the showbenches. Fancy Auriculas, those which do not conform to the accepted groupings and formerly the home of yellow ground Edged varieties and others of failed form, are showing both circularity and proportion. Cliff Timpson's raising, 'Moon Fairy', with its neat tube, solid white paste and cream ground fading out to lilac and mauve is a beautiful addition to the range now seen at the shows. But two new types of auricula have appeared in the past fifty or so years which have added even more to the already wide spectrum of the plant's appeal.

In 1949 Rowland Biffen wrote of the Doubles that 'so rare are they that most Auricula growers have never seen a specimen'. Within ten years, however, things were to change. Border Auricula varieties showing some doubling began to appear in the U.S.A. The flat corolla of the auricula was taking on extra layers of petals and assuming an appearance rather like a ballet dancer's tutu. Progress with any new line of breeding is slow but seeds from the new strains began to arrive in Britain in the 1960s. We are fortunate that the vigour of the Border Auricula persisted and the first few plants increased, as did the number of their offspring. The colouring of the Border Auriculas is more subdued than that of their exhibition relatives and this feature persisted for some time. Pale pinks, creams, yellows and violets dominated the range. Only recently has the persistence of the hybridists persuaded the line to give us blues, oranges, reds and bright yellows. Starting from the American seed lines, the seed house of Barnhaven sold good quality seed which gave a plentiful supply of newcomers to garden borders and the showbenches. By patient and astute crossing from the late 1970s onwards, Gwen Baker, Len Bailey, Derek Salt, Martin Sheader and Ken Whorton continued the flow of new introductions with smooth petals building up into full pips of circular outline. Benefiting from Ken's generosity in distributing both plants and seed, Keith Leeming and Derek Tilt have made their own contributions to the stock of Doubles. Meal has appeared both as a picotee edge and as stippling. The latest breaks have come in the form of stripes. Ken Whorton bred and exhibited a beautiful striped Double called 'Fantasia' which could have come from a Robert Furber illustration of the 1730s. White farina splashed the crimson ground. Derek Salt produced 'Stripey' with its cream and purple mix. On odd occasions nowadays plants of the rare and old 'Mrs. Dargan' appear in public. This is a mixture of red and creamy white striping, generally single, lacking in good form but showing the odd extra petal. It came as something of a shock, therefore, to find no less a figure than David Hadfield, at that time still Secretary of the Northern Section and renowned for his classical Show Auriculas, appearing at the Northern Primula Show at Ossett in Yorkshire in 2003 with a beautiful, completely double truss of the old lady. Ken Whorton had used pollen from 'Mrs. Dargan' in his quest for further Striped Doubles before his death and it may be that it still has more to offer.

A note on the topic of Striped Doubles may serve to illustrate something of the spirit amongst the breeders. In the 1980s I was admiring a plant of 'Singer Stripe' at the Southern Section's London Show. At the end of the afternoon, the breeder, Allan Hawkes, snapped off the winning truss and gave it to me to use as a source of pollen. When put on to my Fancy Auricula, 'Error', it produced several striped seedlings of which only two are commonly grown, the pink and white 'Blackpool Rock' and the purple and white 'Mrs. Davis'. When the latter was crossed with 'Stripey' it gave a small number of ragged seedlings in various shades of purple and white or cream, none fully double, all untidy but all carrying farinaceous stripes. One of these went to Ken Whorton who crossed it with 'Helena Dean'. I received a packet of seed from the cross. This gave rise to numerous, ugly ragamuffins in colours which took in purple, brown, yellow and white. But, standing out in the middle of the seed tray was one squat plant with a thick scape. Its blooms began as light brown streaked with lemon yellow and striped with white meal. As the pips matured, the brown became much darker, leading to its being named 'Brimstone and Treacle'. It is not in the front rank of exhibition Doubles but it has broken colour, mealy stripes and carries pollen. To my mind, it symbolises the spirit of collaboration between the vast majority of growers and hybridists of the present day.

The development of Striped Doubles has been taken still further since the 1990s by Derek Salt who has worked on them quietly and with great determination. Using predominantly plants of his own breeding and then adding a little pollen from 'Brimstone and Treacle', Derek has added a new dimension to this branch of the auricula tribe. He has unostentatiously presented to interested growers double Greens, Greens with stripes of darker green, buff and amber grounds with stripes of mauve and maroon and all overlaid with stripes of farina. The form of these blooms is of the highest quality. Their petals are round, their form is regular and geometrical with plentiful trusses forming a neat hemisphere at the top of strong scapes. These are the plants dreamed of by Rowland Biffen and unheard of by the growers of earlier generations. This achievement ranks amongst the milestones of the auricula.

One last significant step forward in the development of the modern auricula came in the 1960s when Allan Hawkes, already renowned for his Doubles and Gold Centre Alpines, admired a painting of an old Striped Auricula called 'Glory of Chilton' and wondered whether it could be re-created. No Striped Auricula of its type had been known for over one hundred years. He was given an Edged plant with a hint of colour straying up the petals and set to work from there. He then brought into the gene pool a Blue Self with flecks of meal and, again, 'Mrs. Dargan'. One can only marvel at his persistence. After ten years of crossing and re-crossing, striped seedlings began to appear. The body colour was on the dark side of red and was overlaid with stripes of white meal and sometimes flecked with greenish yellow. The outlines of the pips tended to be ragged but odd smoother individuals cropped up. Later, brighter grounds such as the scarlet of 'Marion Tiger' began to appear. 'Arundell Stripe', a mixture of dark blue and yellow but with an angular form and not of the Hawkes breeding line, appeared at the shows. The line was taken up at this point by Derek Parsons of Monmouth. Derek received seed from Allan Hawkes and, from the resulting plants, began a line of breeding which took in nothing from outside. Since the 1990s Derek's amazing plethora of plants has extended the colour range of the type and improved the smoothness and circularity of the pips beyond what many had thought possible. Blue with white mealy stripes, orangey brown with mealy stripes and mauve-pinks with green suffusions are all to be seen on the benches, shown both by the raiser and, as a result of his generosity, by many others. If you spot a Cole Porter song title or a strange name which seems to hide some mysterious or droll significance, it's pretty safe to reckon that it is a Parsons raising.

And so the auricula has come over the last four hundred and fifty years from a simple, mountain flower with a tendency to produce odd aberrations to its present amazing range. After its slow initial development, it has taken on many new forms and colours, especially in the course of the past one hundred and fifty years. Given the spirit of curiosity and openness to new developments amongst modern florists, one can only wonder what the future may hold.

Chapter 2
A LITTLE LIGHT BOTANY

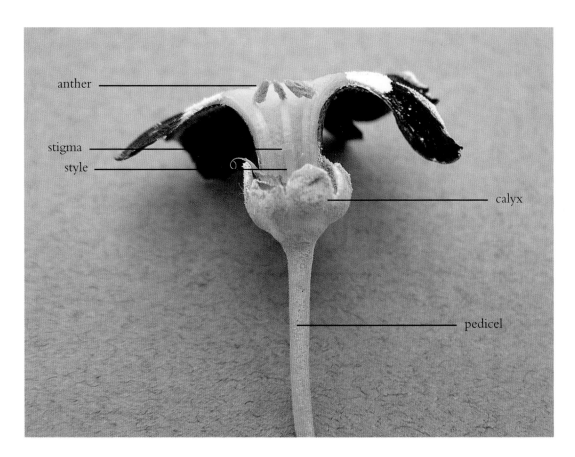

If the story behind the auricula's development has left you with any questions as to what was happening to the blooms, let us now have a closer look at them.

The primula family has flowers which are typically made up of five petals, though in many hybrids they have more than that. The petals join towards the centre of the bloom to form a flat disc known as the corolla. They enclose a tube which runs down from a circular opening in the centre of the corolla. In this tube are the reproductive organs, the anthers which carry the pollen and the style which resembles a pin in shape. The head of this pin is the stigma. This receives the pollen which will help the plant to set seed in the ovaries right at the base of the tube.

The flower sits in a cup of small green leaflets called the calyx, the Latin word for a goblet. This in turn is attached to the footstalk or pedicel. Pedicels join up with the top of the tall stem springing from the base of a leaf. This stem is called the scape.

Primula flowers have a characteristic which

helps them to prosper. Their blooms come in one of two formations. In one, the anthers with their pollen sit at the top of the tube while the style with its stigma lies at the bottom, below the level of the anthers. This formation is known as 'thrum-eyed'. A thrum is a collection of unwoven threads on a loom. In the other layout, the style extends right up to the top of the tube, leaving the stigma at or near the level of the corolla, while the anthers are situated about halfway down the tube. This arrangement is known as 'pin-eyed'. The connection of both terms to the makers of cloth reinforces the old tradition of the auricula's links with the weavers. Plants bear blooms of either one formation or the other, never of both, and each plant carries the same type of flower for the whole of its life. Odd plants can occur where the stigma sits almost level with the anthers at the top of the tube, but they are uncommon and are frowned on by florists.

Throughout the primula tribe, the formation of the blooms aids cross-pollination. If an insect feeds on a thrum-eyed flower, the pollen from the anthers attaches itself to the insect's face. When it visits a pin-eyed type, the pollen rubs off on to the surface of the stigma and pollinates the flower. In the case of a pin-eyed plant, the pollen collects on the insect's proboscis. When it next lands on a thrum-eyed variety, the pollen rubs off on the stigma down the tube.

Although this is nature's way of promoting successful seed production, it is not essential for us to follow it. Since the florists first took up the auricula, the pin eye has been regarded as a fault. Professor Sir Rowland Biffen quotes the phrase 'the pin-eyed flower shows a chasm or vacancy very unpleasant to the eye of the curious florist'. Only thrum-eyed plants are allowed on the showbench, though some growers find the odd pin-eyed seedling attractive or of value for breeding. Some can certainly make a good display in the border, where the gardener is the sole arbiter.

If you should find a pin (as the pin-eyed types are normally referred to by the enthusiasts) which you think might be of value in a breeding line, beware. Pins occur in small numbers when two exhibition varieties of thrum type are crossed. If a pin is deliberately employed as a seed-bearer, the amount of seed which results is greater than in a thrum x thrum cross, but the proportion of pins in the resulting seedlings is likely to be much higher. For showbench plants, only thrum x thrum plants should be considered. Tim Coop raised many unusual and beautiful edged plants with body colours in many shades from a pin x thrum cross, but even nine generations later he was still being plagued by more pin-eyed offspring than were welcome.

Professor Biffen explained that the Edged Show Auricula owes its origins to the ingress of petal tissue, probably from the calyx, into the normal corolla of the pip. It was long believed that this happened around the second quarter of the 1700s and it was accepted that this must have happened all at once. There is now reason to believe that the process came about more gradually with odd flecks and stripes of leaf tissue occurring which then amalgamated into the edges we know today. The paste at the centre of the Edged blooms owed its inception to the farina found at the base of the calyx, Biffen added, and we have no reason to doubt this, though the paste is also found at the centre of blooms on the wild *Primula auricula*. The derivation of the Self-coloured varieties is less clear. Biffen was of the opinion that, given the size and texture of their blooms, they were probably the result of Edged types on which the body expanded and the edge retreated until it finally vanished from the corolla. They do bear some resemblance to the wild *P. auricula* in having a coloured disc with a mealy eye at its centre. Many Self forms also carry the pigmentation which might be expected from *P. hirsuta,* but they do not show the gradation in colouring which can occur in natural hybrids and which is the prominent feature of the Alpine group. No one has left a written record to resolve the enigma. The Alpines themselves were carefully selected variations of the natural hybrid, *P.* x *pubescens.*

As we saw in Chapter One, the Double Auricula of modern times is largely a phenomenon of the second half of the twentieth century. It owes its distinctive form to a notable change. As in other flower families, the reproductive organs developed into extra petals. This occurs most commonly when the anthers become petaloid but leave at the base of the central tube a style which is still capable of producing seed. In some instances the additional petals will continue to carry anthers with pollen at their base. A single extra layer of petals forms an unusual frill round the centre of the pip. If the breeder can hit upon a good cross, an increased degree of doubling will transform the extra layer into several layers, often with a smooth edge and an attractive layout. These layers then build up into a beautiful dome of colour. As doubling becomes more pronounced, the likelihood of pollen being produced becomes increasingly remote and the style shrinks to the point where it is unable to accept fertilisation. In some forms the style may become petaloid without the extra layers of petals sprouting from the anthers. Gwen Baker, a redoubtable champion of the Doubles, often referred to this aberration as 'feather dusters'. Nothing needs to be added to her description. Perfect Doubles occur when both anthers and pistil become petaloid. The blooms so formed are sterile.

Given progress in our understanding of how characteristics are passed on from one generation to the next, it is amazing to think that it is only a little over a hundred years ago that the theory of inheritance was formulated. The idea was put forward by a Czech monk called Gregor Mendel who used two strains of garden peas in his experiments. One strain was tall, the other short. He crossed the two and found all the children of the first generation to be tall. When he intercrossed the new

generation, however, he found on average that, out of four plants, three would be tall and one short. He explained it as follows. Tall plants carried a gene for their height. He called this gene capital T. The dwarf ones had the opposite feature, so he called their gene little t. He thought of the genes as existing in pairs in every pea plant, so all the tall plants had a gene shown as TT. The dwarf ones had a gene called tt. He showed his tall x dwarf cross as:

TT x tt

The offspring of the cross had one gene from each parent. This could be illustrated as:

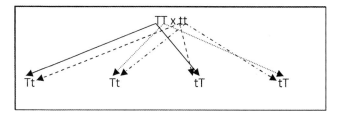

For convenience, both Tt and tT plants are normally shown as Tt. In practice, Mendel found that all these new Tt plants appeared to be tall. He then crossed the offspring amongst themselves. The results are shown below:

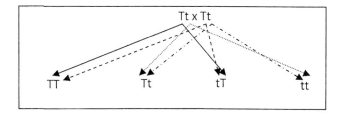

He now had one pure tall plant, two hybrids which appeared tall, but whose offspring could be variable and one pure dwarf form. This was fine for Mendel's dwarf and tall peas but for the auricula breeder things are a little less simple.

The first problem is that auriculas have been bred and selected for so long that no one can be sure whether any characteristic is so pure (as in the tallness of the peas) that it can be relied upon to come through true in its offspring. Self-pollinating any auricula will produce seedlings which are quite different from the parent. The would-be breeder is therefore left to guess what might come from using any particular plant. A good rule of thumb is to talk to several well-known breeders and listen to what they have to say. By pooling their collected advice, a starting point may emerge. It would be futile, on the other hand, to take a plant with a smooth tube and to employ it as a parent in the confident belief that it will bring about a smooth tube in the first or second generation of crossings. That tube might be one of Mendel's Tt peas and pass on the wrong gene to its children. One can just hope that it might happen, but be prepared for many seedlings which lack the desired tube.

One piece of advice, however, is valid: that is to cross within a particular type of plant. If you cross a Gold Centre Alpine with another Gold Centre Alpine you will find that the seedlings generally conform with the type. Likewise a Light Centre x Light Centre cross will throw up mainly Light Centre Alpines. If you cross a Light Centre with a Gold Centre, you will probably end up with some brightly coloured little plants which could grace your garden border but would never be fit to put on a showbench since the eye at the centre of each pip recalls the colour of thin custard.

If, despite all this, you remain the perpetual optimist, you will discover that odd exceptions do occur. 'Roberto', one of the great Green Edges, was the result of a Green x Grey cross. The usual result from such a union is a meal-spattered Green of no quality. Cliff Timpson produced the Double 'Corrie Files' from seed taken from the single-flowered Gold Centre, 'Sirius'. No one has the explanation and both of these cases, it must be stressed, are rarities.

The process of cross-pollination is dealt with in the chapter on cultivation and you may wish to read that before you undertake any serious project, but if all you wish to do is to take some seed from a plant and sow it, then just go ahead with your plan, for many growers in the past have come up with beautiful plants like this. If you have followed the rest of this chapter, however, you will know that you need to be prepared for some disappointments.

Chapter 3
CULTIVATION

The demands of the auricula are essentially very simple. It does not like to be too hot; it does not like to be wet; it likes a little food but not too much. The trouble is that we growers can find it difficult to cope with its simplicity. The plants can be grown out of doors in temperate climates but those with farina on their flowers will be spoiled by any rain which falls on them. The Alpines, having no farina, are a possibility for the open border but they will still need to be split every couple of years to avoid their wasting energy on small offsets which will bear smaller trusses of bloom; and even the Alpines do not always enjoy the temperate but often damp British climate. Some of the richly coloured varieties mark in the rain. To enjoy auriculas at their best, the grower needs to grow them in a pot to be able to savour them at eye level and under some form of cover to keep the blooms at their freshest. The best type of auricula for the rough and tumble of the open garden is the Border Auricula. These have been bred or selected for resilience, freedom of flowering and weather resistance. Their colours are usually more subdued than the exhibition varieties but they can add a touch of refinement to the spring garden.

One advantage of the auricula is that it has never quite forgotten some aspects of its mountain homeland. In these days of high energy prices, it is consoling to know that the auricula does not object to some degree of cold. In my greenhouse while living in north-west England they survived a temperature of 5°F (-15°C) and still flowered the following spring, though a grower in central Shropshire did find that some looked a little the worse for wear after -9.4°F (-23°C). Whilst moving house, I have stood plants under a house wall with a sheet of polythene over them for protection, only to find nearly 6in. (15cm) of snow covering them the next morning. Amongst these plants were several of the Green Edge 'Roberto' which is not always the most amenable. They were moved into a new greenhouse and grew and flowered at the appropriate time in the spring. A few enthusiasts have used a little heat to keep frost off their blooms at flowering time and some have even found artificial lighting to be beneficial, but, for most of us who just want to enjoy the plants' spectacular beauty as nature times it, neither light nor heat is necessary.

A HOME OF THEIR OWN
A greenhouse is the easiest place to grow auriculas, though it is not essential. The craftsmen of the 1800s had little access to the luxury of glass. They provided overhead shelter to their plants with wooden slats or sheets of cloth. A number of today's top-rank growers keep their plants in cold frames. Derek Parsons, the leading breeder of Striped Auriculas, is one of these. His exemplary plants demonstrate that this method of cultivation works. His only caveats are that the grower should not suffer from back problems and should have a reliable supply of warm winter socks. A frame has the advantage of being movable, if it is not too heavy. This may make it possible for you to move your plants to a cooler, shady spot for the summer and back into the light for the autumn, winter and spring. If

you leave your frame standing on terra firma, do make sure that you take some measures such as paving stones or a thick layer of grit to deter earthworms from entering your pots. They do not eat the roots, but they do disturb them by burrowing through the compost. Even today one comes across growers who put a small piece of perforated zinc in the bottom of their pots as a barrier. Anything with a fine mesh which does not decompose too easily might form a suitable barrier.

Slugs and snails are also closer to hand in a frame than is usual in a greenhouse. Any good garden shop or garden centre should be able to provide a means of defence against them. A few growers raise their frames on stands to make them more easily accessible and to avoid problems with pests. Although this adds to the cost, it can be a sensible move. Some form of ventilation from below, such as a slatted base, is a good investment, though you must take care in placing the pots on the slats so that they do not fall over.

If you intend to erect a greenhouse, you need to plan a little beforehand. You must have ready access to water; a canful can become quite a burden if you have to lug it too far or make several trips. Electricity is not essential, though a renowned Secretary of the Northern Section of the National Auricula and Primula Society for over a quarter of a century, and one of the greatest growers and breeders of the auricula, praises the facility. He likes to have a small heater to hand to warm the grower (but not the plants) in the colder months and to enable him to brew tea and listen to Mozart while tending his plants.

Most growers plump for a north-south run if they have a choice in siting a greenhouse. This allows a reasonable exposure to the sun for plants on both sides of the house without either of them having to endure the full glare at the hottest part of the day. Don't worry, if this is not possible, however, for many have grown exhibition specimens in all sorts of situations. Another eminent grower had his greenhouse sited in the gap between his house and his neighbour's. Others have actually opted for a situation where deciduous trees might provide shade in the summer and some protection from wind in the winter. Autumn leaves and falling branches in stormy weather might be a hazard but such a position has its advantages. The situation will govern the time of flowering to some extent but it would be unwise to be too dogmatic about siting. Auricula growers have come up with beautiful plants from some unlikely places.

The size of your greenhouse will depend on your pocket. The usual advice of choosing the biggest one you can afford and accommodate is very sound. You will be able to grow good plants in a 6ft. x 6ft. (2m x 2m) model but cultivation is usually easier in a larger one. Smaller types can become very hot in summer. Before investing all your ready cash, however, consider a couple of other factors. The door needs to be wide enough to permit easy access. It is all too easy to catch the door frame with the edge of a seed tray or, worse still, with a tray full of plants which you have dressed and are just taking out to transport to a show.

You will need some staging on which to stand the plants. Here various stratagems have been employed. All have advantages and disadvantages. Most growers use solid staging. On this they place a layer of grit or sand to keep the base of the pots just moist and to prevent the air rising round the plants from becoming too dry. Some deploy several inches of sand and plunge the pots. This is useful if you decide to use clay pots, since any water in the sand helps to prevent loss of moisture through the sides of the pot. If you opt for plunging the pots in sand, you need to be wary of any build-up of pests in the plunge material and change it every year or so. If you spread the old material on the garden in the autumn or winter, the weather will kill off the majority of nasties. Once the sand on the bench is dry for the winter, it provides insulation for the roots in very cold spells. Other growers prefer a layer of moist peat or soilless potting compost under the pots. This serves much the same purpose as the sand and is considerably lighter and may be changed every year to forestall any build-up of pests or disease. For either method, make sure the material on the benches does not become too wet and be careful when lifting pots from the substrate. It is all too easy to allow a blob of it to fall on adjacent plants, another potential disaster when everything is at the peak of bloom. Granulated materials such as Hortag are expensive but hold a good amount of water. Capillary matting has been used by a few growers but its water retention is so efficient that any pots in direct contact with it are apt to become waterlogged and most florists avoid it.

Few growers opt for slatted staging in a greenhouse, since it demands great care not to place a pot so close to a gap between the slats that it topples over. The air round the plants also tends to be drier which encourages red spider mite. And yet this was the form used by Richard Westwood to produce some of the best plants of the 1990s right up to his untimely death in 2006. Each of his clay pots stood in a saucer and water was poured into the saucer, never on the top of the compost. He also took care to damp down the floor. This method must have demanded enormous time and attention, in addition to a thorough knowledge of the varieties being grown, but from it came some of the most superb plants seen on the showbench. For the beginner it is not a path to go down, but, if you have such flair and dedication, the proof that it works stands in the records of the National Auricula and Primula Society.

Adequate ventilation is essential for healthy plants. Most off-the-shelf green-houses come with the minimum of ventilators, often just one in the roof. Auriculas do not mind the cold, but they do not thrive if the greenhouse becomes too hot and dry or tropically humid. Try to stretch your funds to provide at least one roof vent on each side and more if you can. Louvres at the far end and round the walls are much to be recommended. Any air which enters through the door can then blow down the length of the house and across the plants. If the weather should be wet or if a snow shower threatens on a bright spring day, the louvres will permit the air to move through the house and still preserve your beauties from any damage by the elements. If you plan to keep your plants in the greenhouse throughout the year (and many leading growers prefer to put them outside in shaded areas for the summer), it is not a good idea to purchase a greenhouse which uses tall, single sheets of glass for the sides. It is far more useful to have smaller, overlapping panes, so that the upper row of glass may be removed in the hotter months and a length of netting pinned in the gap. This permits a good flow of air and keeps out unwelcome insects.

One final consideration in selecting your greenhouse and staging is that of work and storage areas. You need adequate space to store clean pots, seed trays, compost, used items ready for washing, an area where you can work and re-pot, a space for all the bits and pieces you will need such as labels and a pencil and also a small area close to hand where you can put a cup of tea or coffee, for a cuppa with your beautiful auriculas is a little bit of perfection.

POTS

The growers of the eighteenth and nineteenth centuries often used clay pots which are depicted as considerably larger than those favoured today. They then deposited a thick layer of drainage material in the bottom so that the plants were essentially growing in the equivalent of a wide bowl. Some of the composts advocated at the time would have needed all the drainage available. Today's composts are simpler and freer draining; consequently smaller pots are preferred. A mature plant will grow in a 3½in. pot (a number 9F in metric terms). Good offsets need a 3in. (8cm) and smaller ones a 2½in. (6cm). Clay pots are expensive and demand great care in handling. They retain less moisture than plastic pots which means more care in summer but less risk of excessive wet in the winter. Despite this porosity, clay pots still benefit from some drainage material at the bottom or a piece of broken pot at the base to prevent the compost from washing out of the relatively large drainage hole. It is also possible to find a type of pot called a Long Tom made of clay. These are considerably taller than the usual type and provide extra room for compost and long roots. When well presented on a showbench in pristine condition, they look elegant, but salt deposits, chips and dirt can easily mar their appearance and they are better suited to the experienced grower. All clay pots need to be kept clean as they easily become slimy and slippery. Between uses they need to be soaked for a day or so to soften any stubborn dirt or chalky deposits on the surface and then scrubbed vigorously. A wire brush may be necessary to remove the most persistent accretions.

Most modern florists choose to grow in plastic pots. They are cheaper and easier to handle. You may prefer to use square plastics of the smaller sizes to bring on small plants and offsets, as they accommodate more compost than their round equivalents and can touch each other on the staging, but you should be aware that the tradition, and sometimes the rules, state that plants go on the showbench in round, terracotta coloured pots only.

COMPOSTS

If you are in the company of auricula growers, make sure that you have adequate time in hand before you mention the word 'compost'. It is a much vexed subject and each will have his or her views. The obnoxious mixtures advocated in the past are, fortunately, laughed at today. Experience has shown that the auricula needs a free-draining mixture which will retain the small amount of nutrient it needs. Finding such a medium is not always easy.

Before the days of ready-bagged compost from the garden centre, a good open loam was mixed with silver sand, grit and leafmould or peat. The best loam was reckoned to come from just below a good pasture or from molehills. The latter is still used by some growers today. Mixtures of this sort are best left to those with a lot of experience, for the wrong sort of loam and any disease organisms not removed by sterilisation could wreak havoc in the confines of a pot.

The John Innes Potting Compost Number 2 served for many years as the standard mixture for auriculas. This is a mixture of loam, sand and fertiliser available in 4 grades, seed, 1, 2 and 3, with various proportions of sand and fertiliser according to the grade. If you should find a reliable version today, it is a great boon. Unfortunately, even with a badge from the John Innes Association, there is too much variation in what comes out of the bags; indeed even the same brand has been known to vary from one year to the next. It would seem that there is no reliable and permanent source of good loam to act as a base. The advent of soilless composts seemed to offer new possibilities to the auricula and initial results were promising. The food reserves of such mixtures are soon used up, however, and a judicious feeding regime is essential. Plants become too blowsy if overfed. They can also drown if the grower uses plastic pots and is a little heavy-handed with the watering can. Even soilless composts are now showing too much inconsistency for many growers. It is not uncommon for some bags to contain large lumps or long strings of unshredded material. An open, nicely fibrous mix is the ideal.

If you can find a good loam-based compost, it needs a little extra drainage material such as coarse sand or fine grit, unless it is already based on a sandy loam. You should not ram down the soil in the pots and be aware too that the compost consolidates if you water constantly from the top. If the compost should become too compacted, you run the risk of damaging the roots. An open texture is the ideal. The compost will retain nutrients for a considerable time and extra feed will be needed on only two or three occasions during the growing year. It is essential to keep an eye on the pots in the course of the summer, however, as they will dry out quite readily, especially if you are using clay pots.

One medium which has been found to be effective by many growers is a mixture of John Innes No. 2 and a good soilless compost with added drainage. The usual formula is about five measures of J.I., three measures of soilless and two measures of drainage material. This formula is not fixed. Good plants are grown in mixtures of equal measures of the two proprietary composts with the added drainage. It will depend largely on the quality of the two chief components and then on the grower's ability to handle the ensuing mixture, for no two individuals treat their plants in the same way. The aim should be a growing medium which can be felt to be damp but not wet after any watering has had a chance to drain away. A recent innovation which has been seen with some superb prize-winning plants is the use of Perlite as the drainage material. This white, crumbly substance is a heat-treated form of pumice. It is so light that it

will float on water, yet it retains a porous structure which enables tiny amounts of air to remain in the compost without too much danger of drying out the roots. Tom Rapley, an eminent grower from the north-east of England, has put some beautiful examples of difficult plants on the showbenches using this method. Other growers have been so impressed by this success that they are experimenting with Perlite in their potting mixes. Though not cheap, at the time of writing it is only marginally more expensive than good grit which is becoming increasingly difficult to find. Excellent plants have appeared at recent shows grown in a compost made up of four measures of John Innes No. 2, two measures of good quality soilless compost and two measures of Perlite. The measure used should be by capacity, not weight, so you may choose to use a litre pot filled to the brim as one measure. The resulting medium has a good crumb structure with the soil to carry some nutrients, the soilless compost to retain moisture and the Perlite allowing an essential supply of air to the roots. The moisture in the other two ingredients prevents them from drying out and water is taken up easily either from standing the pot in water or supplying it from above.

The moisture level in any pot is an awkward thing to gauge. It used to be maintained that the best gadget to assess moisture was a good grower's thumb. Not all of us are blessed with an accurately calibrated thumb so you may wish to stir the very top of the compost to see how it looks just below, while taking great care not to go down to any depth at which the roots may be growing. Experience is a great boon in assessing whether your plants need water. Some growers can even gauge the state of their compost from the weight of the pot. The soundest advice is that, if you are unsure, don't. This is especially true in the heat of the summer, the late autumn, during the winter months and up to the beginning of growth. When auriculas are in active growth during the spring and the early part of the summer, they do not like to go dry. Over the hottest months it is regrettably all too easy to permit them to desiccate or to overwater and allowance should be made for the heat before water is given.

Another option is a moisture meter. These little devices have a prong which is inserted into the soil and a dial which gives the grower a measure of the compost's water content. Unfortunately, they vary greatly in their accuracy and the prong may damage important roots, but, if you should find yourself the owner of one of these gadgets, they can prove useful, provided that you do not take any advice given on the packaging relating to 'primulas' as appropriate for auriculas. I have owned two of these devices and always used quite a low number on the scale (just above dryness, in fact) as a benchmark for watering. It would appear that the 'primula' recommendation in the instructions on the packaging must have been worked out with some quite thirsty primroses or candelabra primulas in mind.

POTTING-ON AND RE-POTTING

If you have some plants, some form of shelter for them, a good stock of clean pots and some compost, it is time to look at what we do to get them started.

You will also need labels and a pencil, scissors or a pocket knife in case any roots are damaged or overly long and – preferably – some methylated spirit or domestic bleach in which to clean the cutting tools. Some experienced growers also like to have a small amount of either flowers of sulphur or ground charcoal with which to dress any wounds they may have to inflict on the plants. You may also choose to employ a fungicide such as Dithane 945 if there is any sign of disease on the roots. If you use insecticides, a sprayer containing a suitable aphid-killer may come in handy. Pot-

washing is not a pleasant chore but it is essential to get it done before you even contemplate moving your plants. Next, choose a spot where you have adequate space to put your clean and dirty pots without getting them mixed up. A container or neat heap of fresh compost nearby is more comfortable than having to bend down for each new handful. Finally have some form of receptacle such as a bucket or bag for the old compost, bits of foliage and root and any small offsets which will come off the plant as you work on it. You can get through the task without all this preparation but you will find the task easier and quicker if you think it all through in advance.

Potting-on is moving a plant from a small pot to a larger one. It usually involves the bare minimum of root disturbance, though most growers like to remove a little of the old compost from the sides and the top surface of the rootball. It is a straightforward and quite enjoyable task.

Remove the plant from its pot by forming a V shape with the index finger and the middle finger of one hand. You then place the V round the collar of the plant, using your thumb and remaining fingers to cover the compost. If you now turn the pot upside down, the plant should slide out of its old pot. If it refuses, tap the rim of the inverted pot gently on a firm surface. This will usually free it. Plastic pots may be squeezed lightly too, though not enough to disturb the ball of soil. If the roots are beginning to fill the pot and curling round the base of the compost, it is time to move the plant into a bigger pot. If not, remove a little of the compost from the base of the roots, put a small amount of fresh compost into a clean pot of the same size and put the plant back for another spell. Scraping some of the old compost from round the collar and replacing it with fresh will help to feed the plant, and also remove any moss which might be forming there and make the whole thing look neater. One

Plant removed from old pot

Ready to insert into clean pot

Filling with compost

Topped up and tapped down

annoying trait of some cultivars is the production of numerous offsets around or just below the collar. If allowed to grow, they will detract from the overall vigour of the plant. Remove these with either a sharp knife or your thumbnail, leaving just one or two in an accessible position in case the original specimen decides to rot off. Applying a little flowers of sulphur or powdered charcoal was the traditional precaution against disease setting in through the wounds which ensue.

If the plant has grown well enough to merit a bigger pot, put a little fresh compost into the new home. Now place the old root ball on top of it and make sure that there is still sufficient space at the top to add a further layer of compost in the future when the carrot begins to extend upwards still further. Then add your compost slowly round the sides of the rootball, tapping the pot gently on the working surface to settle it down and leave no large air gaps round the edge. You may find any small utensil such as an old spoon helps in the job of filling up the pot. When the compost reaches the leaves at the collar, tap the plant on the bench again, make sure that it is correctly labelled and put the pot in a tray or tub of water, allowing adequate time for it to soak up through the compost. Only when the surface glistens with the moisture should you remove the pot and stand it in a cool, shady place until growth recommences. If the weather is not too hot, it will not need more water for some time.

Larger plants need to be re-potted annually. Occasionally one comes across growers who leave some plants in the same compost for two years but they are in a small minority. The time for re-potting is an area of much discussion. Florists of the nineteenth century were sometimes dogmatic about the exact dates for commencing. Modern growers generally prefer to undertake the task either immediately after the shows or at the tail end of the summer. The arguments advanced by both groups are sensible and fine plants are produced by both schools of thought. The U.K. May-June re-potters will tell you that the plants are growing strongly and their roots will recover from the shock before the height of summer when the plants do not grow. The July-August group argue that, provided you choose a cool period, the plants will start their new period of growth in fresh compost with all the pests which may have taken up residence over the main run of summer removed. The plants may then continue their growth uninterrupted through the cooler autumn weather. It is reassuring, however, to hear some outstanding growers admit that, either

through choice or necessity, they have re-potted plants at most times of the year except the very hottest and coldest, though they like to start after the shows. Most florists have been forced to re-pot damaged or diseased plants out of the usual season and know that it is possible to produce reasonable results afterwards. There is no scientific proof to support either opinion. Local climate and the grower's personal inclination will point each individual towards their preferred time.

Remove the plant to be re-potted from its old container by putting your fingers round the neck, as described earlier, and inverting the pot. Again, a gentle squeeze of the pot or a light tap of the rim against a firm surface should free the rootball, allowing the plant to slide out. The advice given in the past was that all of the old compost should be removed. Most present-day growers prefer to loosen the growing medium from the outer half of the roots. You will find that gentle combing with your fingers from the base of the rootball will suffice with the majority of plants. If the compost is firm amongst the roots, you might have to tap it gently against the side of the waste bucket or rake it lightly with a dibber or plant label to loosen it. Allow the top layer of compost to fall away from the surface too.

Once the roots are laid bare, look at them closely for any signs of disease or damage. Trim off any which are not perfect and treat any which are carrying aphids. These are rare nowadays since the advent of systemic insecticides but their characteristic white fluff on the roots was dreaded by growers fifty years ago. Next look at the carrot (the main root stem). If there is any sign of die-back at the base, cut it off at a point where you can see healthy white material. If the carrot is over-long, again trim it back but make sure that there are sufficient roots left to sustain the plant over the coming months. Any rot in the carrot needs to be dug out carefully. If you have any offsets or emerging

Top left: Plant showing fresh roots and ready to be potted on

Top right: Some old compost removed

Above: Fitted into new pot

Right: Topped up and tapped down

buds, either from the carrot or round the neck of the plant, now is a good chance to remove them. Any offset about 2in. (5cm) or more in length might produce a new plant, especially if it possesses a root or two of its own. Cut these off and lay them aside to pot up presently. Any buds need a little consideration. You may care to leave the odd bud to provide an offset or two next year. You may also wish to remove the lot in order to produce a single-crowned plant for exhibition, though you may have to remove some small buds or offsets again just prior to putting it on the showbench. This is a good time to treat any cut surfaces with flowers of sulphur to keep out disease and to clean your cutting tools with the methylated spirits or bleach.

Now take a clean pot, put a small amount of compost in the base and lower the plant into the pot. The collar needs to sit about ½in. (1-1.5cm) below the level of the rim, somewhere around where one usually finds the lower rim inside modern plastic pots. Add the fresh compost gently, pouring it round the edge of the rootball and amongst the roots. Tap the pot gently on the bench every now and then to settle the compost and avoid air holes in which the roots might dry out and where they will certainly find neither food nor water. When the compost reaches the level of the collar, tap the pot gently again, label the plant (you may find it useful to put a date on the reverse) and then water it, preferably by plunging it in a pan of water reaching well up the pot, even to the level of the compost. When the surface gleams with moisture, remove it and place the pot in a cool, shady place for a couple of weeks to allow the roots to gain a purchase on the new growing medium.

Any offsets taken in the course of re-potting can be potted up in either a 2½in. (6cm) pot, a tray of modules or several of the same type can be inserted round the edge of a 3in. (8cm) pot. Any particularly weak ones might survive if you put them in a pot of pure horticultural sand and take great pains to keep them moist. Again, label them clearly.

HYBRIDISING

This is a fascinating pursuit. The odds against coming up with a classic new cultivar are huge, but the majority of keen growers attempt to defy the mathematics and add to the roll of honour. If you wish to try your hand at raising new varieties, watch the mature plants carefully as they flower in spring (April and May in the U.K.). You need to see a good supply of pollen on the anthers of the male parent and a glistening appearance on the stigma of the seed bearer indicating that the pollen is likely to adhere. Offsets will sometimes carry pollen or bear seeds but more often they do not have the energy reserves required. It can be very disappointing to watch a seed pod form in May or early June, change colour at high summer and then in the autumn turn out to be empty. A strong mature plant is a much safer bet.

Various ways have been found to transfer the pollen from the donor to the recipient. The one most commonly employed is to take a small but sharp pair of scissors and snip off the corolla of the mother plant below the anthers but avoiding the stigma. This will leave the stigma easily accessible. Another way to achieve the same end is to hold the edge of the pip on either side and gently tear the bloom open, so leaving a vertical tear down the tube and the stigma again exposed to receive pollen. Then take a pair of fine tweezers, remove an anther from the pollen parent and brush the stigma gently on the stigma of the seed parent. Wash the scissors and the tweezers in methylated spirits to kill any stray pollen or unsuspected traces of disease. If you can afford to use more than one pip in your pollination, it is wise to do so. There is no guarantee that any cross will take. There is much discussion as to whether one should also make the reverse cross (so that the roles of pollen parent and seed parent are reversed) and no firm scientific evidence as to whether this is necessary with auriculas, but it might be worth the little extra effort. Some experienced hybridists

Above: A bloom which has been cut off with scissors just above the stigma, so exposing the stigma.

Top right: A bloom being torn in half to leave the stigma open to receive pollen.

Right: An anther carrying pollen being applied to the stigma.

always recommend a reverse cross. When you have completed your crosses on any plant, identify it in some way. You may wish to tie a small piece of cotton or wool round the footstalk of the pips which you have pollinated. You may also put a label in the pot. Experience adds that a reliable paper record of some sort is advisable. It is so easy to lose track of the parentage of any cross.

All you can do now is to watch and wait. If your cross is successful, the base of the flower will swell and the growing seed pod will burst through the base of the tube. As the summer progresses, it will reach a maximum size and stop growing. After this it slowly turns a straw-colour. The whole process takes about three months. When the pedicel also begins to take on this straw shade, snip it off and either separate the seed from the softer material underneath before storing it in a paper envelope or put the whole pod in an envelope and wait for the seed to fall out. The seed should be brown and hard. Any that are small and soft are unlikely to be viable, though it is unwise with auriculas ever to be dogmatic, for it is not unknown for unripe seed to germinate. The translucent envelopes formerly used by stamp collectors were ideal for seed

Above: Seedlings germinating.

Top right: Seedlings pricked out.

Right: Seedpods.

storage but are now both expensive and hard to come by.

If you should intend to try your hand at breeding new varieties, the Midlands Section of the National Auricula and Primula Society publishes a little booklet by Derek Parsons, the raiser of so many outstanding varieties. It is called *Raising New Varieties of Auriculas.* The tiny size of this publication belies its truly excellent quality. It is inexpensive, simple and entertaining to read and packed with the wisdom of many years of successful breeding. Purchase a copy, if you can.

SEED AND SEEDLINGS

No single view on the best time to sow auricula seed prevails. Some growers sow seed immediately it ripens; some store it in an airtight jar in a domestic fridge until early autumn; others again keep the seed in a good container in the fridge and wait until early in the New Year or just a little later before they sow. A small seed tray of any good seed compost suffices in either case. Wet it thoroughly (you may care to use a little fungicide to do so) and then allow it to drain. When it is nicely moist (and this may require waiting until the next day), sprinkle the seeds across the surface, ensuring that they are not too crowded. This will make the task of pricking them out easier later on. On no account should you cover the seeds with a substantial layer of compost. They need light to germinate. A thin scattering of Vermiculite may be applied to keep the surface moist. You may also wait until tiny roots or seed leaves begin to emerge before adding either the Vermiculite or a fine sprinkling of compost. Make sure that the seeds do not become too hot. Many of the primula family go back to sleep if subjected to too much warmth; they then wait for the coolness of spring to revive them. If the seeds should be frosted, do not worry. They will come through being frozen into the compost. Being allowed to dry out is their main hazard. Should there be any danger of the tray or pot drying out, stand it in a sufficient depth of water to wet the surface. A watering can may disturb the seeds too much, though a hand spray used with caution can keep the surface just moist. The danger with this device is that the compost below may dry out without being visible and the dryness under the surface cause damage to the newly emerging roots. Forceful spraying may also cause the top of the compost to form a crust which can prevent any seeds caught inadvertently below it from pushing through.

Autumn sowing often produces some seedlings before the winter brings growth to a halt but you must wait until later the following spring before you do anything else. More seeds will sprout with the increasing light and warmth but do allow time for germination to proceed. Auriculas will not be hurried.

Winter or early spring sowing leads to germination getting under way with the better weather. Again allow plenty of time for the seed to wake up. As soon as the seedlings have formed a strong pair of seed leaves or their first tiny pair of true leaves, prick them out into a compost specifically designed for seedlings or young plants. John Innes Potting Compost No. 1 is the appropriate soil-based type. A soilless version where the bag states specifically that it is suitable for seedlings is an alternative. A third possibility is a mix of three measure of John Innes, two measures of soilless compost and two measures of Perlite or grit. Prick out the seedlings into seed trays filled with compost, leaving just over 1in. (3cm) between each seedling. Handle them very carefully by the leaves; pressing on the stem can cause irrevocable damage. Seed modules are very useful here – the seedlings are all together and convenient to handle. The modules also make the later removal of the young plants an easier task. Settle them in gently by immersing the tray or module in water up to the level of the new compost and put them in a cool place to send out fresh roots. Growth will vary now. Some batches of seedlings rush to form new, young plants. Others take much more time. Wait until you can see roots all around the compost before you pot them on into larger homes. A 3in. (8cm) pot will normally suffice. Square pots of any size hold more compost than the round version of the same nominal measurement. They also fit snugly together which is an advantage if you then put the pots into a rectangular tray. Larger plastic modules with twenty-four cells to each one also suffice to bring the plants to bloom. Some seedlings will send up flowers in these pots or modules; others will wait for another season and need a bigger pot before they produce their first truss.

CARING FOR AURICULAS

So, if you have some plants, adequate pots and compost, a safe home for your treasures and a knowledge of basic procedures, how do you care for them? Let us take the year step by step and look for potential high and low points.

Winter

The old growers used to say that the auricula had two seasons of growth, one just after the longest day and another after the shortest day. They were right. The calendar might begin in January, but the auricula recognises a slightly different organisation of things. The old hands know that nothing much will happen in the dark months, but if you should see a slight change in the brightness of colour of the leaves or the remaining cone of foliage during January and the first half of February, enjoy it as a precursor to the pleasures to come. The pots should not need much water, but if they are dry, do not dribble a little on the surface. Make sure that the water reaches all the compost and then allow the pot to drain. Carefully remove any leaves which die off or show any sign of mould or die-back; tweezers might be useful in tackling the job at this time of year. If you use them to grasp the bottom of the leaf blade near the stem and roll them down towards the soil, the most tenacious leaves will usually come away without damage. Should you notice any signs of rot, either on the stem or the leaves, remove it at once, even if it means cutting into the carrot (the main root). This may lead to the demise of the plant if the incision is too deep, but you may rest assured that rot left to its own devices will kill off the plant. It is advisable to treat the cut surface with a fungicide.

Sow seeds at any suitable time this season. January is a month favoured by many growers.

If severe frost is threatened, a layer of horticultural fleece or newspaper placed gently over the top of the plants gives a little protection, but remember that auriculas are very hardy.

Check that there are no drips from the roof of your greenhouse or the top of your frame. Seal any chinks you find.

Make sure you have a satisfactory supply of clean pots and labels to hand. At the end of the winter keep an eye open for fresh stocks of potting compost arriving in the shops. Do not be tempted by old stock which may have deteriorated.

Spring

As the days extend, the leaves will start to spread out from the overwintering central cone. The plants will begin to assume a brighter look. Mealy leaves peeling back in this way will seem almost white and the smell of the farina, which resembles for many noses that of incense, will become one of the delights on entering the greenhouse or lifting the frame lid on a sunny morning. Do not be in a hurry to water too much at this point. Wait until the compost is drying out and then wet it carefully, taking care not to mark the foliage. This is the time of year when many growers like to give a feed of some sort, usually a balanced fertiliser, to encourage early growth. Too much fertiliser will promote over-vigorous leaf growth at the expense of well-shaped flowers. Keep a wary eye on any plants which you might intend to exhibit. As the season progresses, you may have to put them into more sunlight or into a shady spot to speed up or slow down their development. Make sure that you keep them away from any places where rain may drip on them or wind blow them about. At all times, make sure that the plants are kept as cool as possible and maintain a good flow of air across them.

You can take offsets from any plants which are offering them, provided they are mature enough to throw roots. If you do this carefully, you will still be able to exhibit the plant at one of the shows. Any offset of 1½-2in. (4–5cm) with a few roots may be put into a 2½in. (6cm) pot. Many growers use plastic modules set in trays to accommodate offsets of this size. They find it easier to handle a whole tray than individual, smaller pots. Rooted offsets from last year should be potted on now, if you can see a good show of roots round the sides and base of the soil ball. Move them on to the next size up but do not be in too much of a hurry to get them into their final 3½in. (9cm) pots. If they are unable to take up the water which you put on them, the compost may become stagnant and cause the roots to rot.

Keep an eye open also for any pests which may appear and take appropriate measures.

April and May are the crown of the year (in the U.K), for your plants will come into bloom. Although they will stand up without support, the scapes look more orderly if you keep them bolt upright with a fine piece of wood such as a barbecue skewer. These are thinner and less prone to splinters than the old lengths of split bamboo. Secure the top of the scape to the support with a short piece of fine material such as wool or thin string, making sure that you run the tie between the scape and the support to prevent chafing. Allow a little slack so that there is no danger of the stem being cut or restricted. An alternative to the wooden stake is a length of wire with its top ½in. (1cm) bent at 90° to the main run. This small piece is then bent again to form a U shape into which the top of the scape will fit. Wire supports of this type have the advantage of being raised easily in the compost as the scape extends upwards. If you intend to show a plant, it may help to insert a small piece of cotton wool into the footstalks to spread the truss out into a regular formation. Should you not intend to exhibit, just wait for one of the most beautiful displays which the world of flowers has provided.

If you would like to try your hand at raising new varieties, now is the time. New plants are always needed, as the useful life of an auricula can be just three or four years and is generally no more than fifty years, though there are some notable exceptions. Select plants from the same group, such as two Grey Edges or two Light Centred Alpines. Few good plants arise from crosses between dissimilar groups.

Now is also the time to examine critically any seedlings which might be coming into flower for the first time. If they are not up to the standard of their parents, then consider giving them as presents to friends who are less of a florist than yourself, planting them in your own garden if they are weatherproof or just putting them on the compost heap. It can be painful and sometimes dispiriting to get rid of the vast majority of your little treasures; if so, get a critical friend to give you some advice or to do the job for you. It is too easy to end up with a collection of near misses which never quite make the grade. One recent aid in the selection of promising seedlings is the digital camera. If you take a picture of anything showing promise, you can compare it with others which bloom later before taking an irrevocable step. But, if against some pretty steep odds you come up with a good plant, think of the joy of naming it.

Above all at this time of year, explain to friends that you are not being antisocial if they do not see you around as much as they expect. They might even appreciate an invitation to look at your plants.

In the U.K. shows both large and small take place from mid-March to mid-May. They provide a good opportunity to see on display plants from the country's most skilled growers and breeders, to join one of the three sections of the National Auricula and Primula Society and also to purchase plants from the sales tables where you will find varieties, both old and new, at very reasonable prices. Plant sales are an important source of income for all the sections of the National Auricula and Primula Society. The plants on offer are the products of the members themselves; they take a half of the price you pay, the other half going to the Society. You will still pay less than the market rate and you will have access to varieties not often available on the open market. You will also be able to meet and talk to those who have just discovered auriculas and to some of the most experienced figures in the auricula world. Most will gladly give of their time to help and advise. Breeders are also more open in talking about their crosses than was the case in the last century when the parentage of new varieties was often a very closely guarded secret. There is much to be gained from a very small subscription to at least one of the three sections of the Society. Show days are a high point in the auricula year.

Summer

The first task at the beginning of summer is to enjoy the last of the blooms. The plants will continue to expand their leaves and to ripen seed. Re-potting needs to be undertaken at some time over the next three months.

Think about which varieties you would like more of and which to reduce in number next season. If your memory is likely to miss out on small details, keep a paper record near your plants but try to remember to date each entry. If you decide to re-pot mature plants now, wait for a time when the weather forecast is predicting a cooler spell.

Now is also the time to consider moving your plants outside, if that is your intention for the year. As long as you can keep the plants cool and prevent them from becoming soggy, they will appreciate this. If your auriculas are to remain in the greenhouse over the summer, keep as much air flowing over them as possible. Open the vents, keep the door open and, if possible, remove some glass from the sides of the greenhouse. If you secure some green netting along the sides, this will keep out many insect pests and birds.

Check over the plants regularly looking for any signs of pests and disease and take appropriate measures.

If your auriculas are exposed to bright sunshine for more than an hour or two each day, provide some shade for them. In a greenhouse or frame the green plastic netting sold for the purpose is very useful. A single layer is usually adequate, though two may be needed in a really open position. Another solution is an application of a white reflective liquid such as Coolglass which is painted on in spring and brushed off in early autumn. A luxury solution comes in the form of roller blinds attached to the exterior of a greenhouse. A cheap, emergency remedy is to cover the plants with a single layer of newspaper or horticultural fleece, but do not leave this on longer than necessary. Both materials can hold in the heat.

Watering is one of the prime difficulties this season. As temperatures rise, the roots of the auricula become less active. If the plants lose water through their leaves, they may not take up the same quantity through their roots and the foliage will flag. Now is the time to give that little extra attention to the water content of your compost. If your thumb or other meter indicates any normal level of moisture, do not be tempted to pour on more water. Wait for the cool of the evening when the plants may recover of their own accord as soon as root activity recommences. A fine, overhead spray from a sprayer filled with cold water will help to cool them down and add just a little dampness to the atmosphere which will deter red spider mite. You might also water the floor of the greenhouse early in the morning. Although the auricula does not care for a swampy atmosphere, its wild ancestors were accustomed to the morning mists of the Alps. Should the compost genuinely be dry, water it thoroughly. Plunging the pots in a container with water up to the level of the top of the compost will not cause as much compaction as overhead watering.

If you use a watering can, apply the water carefully through as small a nozzle as possible. There are various solutions to this difficulty. One is to use a small watering can which you will need to top up frequently from an adjacent supply of water, or even from a larger can. You could even use an old teapot as we are told the House of Douglas did. A more modern gadget which has been found genuinely useful is a full size watering can with a button situated just above the handle. This is attached to a valve in the spout. By pressing the button with care the grower can provide a gentle stream of water to any pot, particularly those at the rear of the staging, without any danger of flooding it or its neighbours. This will keep the compost open and help to keep the surface from panning.

If you are in any doubt about watering, don't. It is better to wait until you are sure that you should.

Danger arises at this time of year if the plants are left unattended for a lengthy spell. If you have a gardening friend (especially a fellow florist) who might have a look at your collection, offer mutual assistance. If you can keep your plants cool while you are away, they will survive for several days, especially if any form of shade can be provided. If they do dry out despite all precautions, water thoroughly and await the results. If you are lucky, the leaves will become turgid again and the plants continue to grow. If they do not, some will turn yellow and die off leaving some sturdy green foliage to grow on but later a constriction will appear around the collar of the plant. Some build up again to their previous size in a year or two, some will send out a supply of fresh offsets while

the main crown withers, but some unfortunately will just die off.

Watch for ripening seed pods as the summer progresses and decide whether to sow seeds immediately or to wait until January. (An alternative is to sow some now and keep the rest for a New Year sowing.)

If you chose to delay your re-potting or if you did not complete all the pots earlier, any spells when the weather forecast predicts cooler weather during the summer can be a good time to tackle the task. Mid- to late August is a favourite of some British growers, if the weather is not too hot. By the time that the roots have settled into the new compost, daytime temperatures should be down to a more temperate mark and the plants will still have some time to bulk up a little before the autumn shuts down growth for the year.

Autumn
After the late growth which follows the longest day, auriculas begin to slow down. The older leaves which have done their job will begin to turn yellow. A little yellow here and there should not worry you. Wait until the bulk of a leaf looks out of sorts before you try to detach it. Hold as much of the collar as you can before you pull the leaf sharply from one side to the other. Should you fail to hold the plant securely, there is a danger that you may break off the crown if the leaf is not ready to come away freely. When a leaf insists on remaining attached, do not force it, leave it for a day or so longer. Foliage showing signs of rot should not be allowed to stay on. If the sideways tug does not loosen the leaf's grip on the main stem, two more lines of action offer themselves. One is to cut off the rotting section and allow the remainder to stay attached for a time in the hope that it will come away cleanly later. You will need to look at the leaf regularly in case further rot sets in on the cut section. The other course is to grasp the very

base of the leaf blade with a long pair of tweezers and roll it downwards, though again paying heed that it does not snap the main stem. This will leave a fresh scar where the leaf has been growing which some growers like to treat with flowers of sulphur to help the wound to dry and to try to prevent the entry of disease. The mould which grows on auricula leaves, if left, can easily spread from the dying tissue on to living foliage with which it comes into contact.

Keep the ventilation going. Water with caution as the days shorten. With reduced growth and transpiration the plants need less moisture and roots will object to sitting in soggy compost. Wait until the plant really needs water and then ensure that the whole pot is moistened.

If you have kept your auriculas outside for the summer, bring them in under the protection of frame or greenhouse some time during the autumn. They now need to be kept drier.

If you are a member of any sections of the National Auricula and Primula Society, try to get to the Annual General Meeting where you will have the opportunity to play your part in the development of the society and to hear how others have fared during the year. It is also the place at which offsets of new plants are distributed and received. If you have shown anything of quality at the earlier shows, you may be lucky enough to have a small plant of a newer variety put into your hands. Alternatively, you may also have a chance to enquire about the availability of any which caught your eye on the showbench.

A glance at the show results from the 1960s and '70s will reveal that there was a flow of good, new varieties on the showbenches, but many of the old names persisted. In the years since then the quality of many new introductions steadily improved, especially amongst the Alpines, Doubles and Stripes. Any list of named cultivars will almost certainly become outdated in quite a short time. Nevertheless, if you are looking for a few types to acquire, either from a reliable commercial source or at Society plant sales, the following chapter on varieties is offered as a guide.

Chapter 4
An Alphabetical List of Varieties

In most writings on the auricula, varieties are listed according to their individual type, so all Green Edges are together, followed by Grey Edges, then White Edges, with similar divisions for the Selfs and Alpines. Such an arrangement permits the reader to compare the views of the author on each plant and good photographs may permit the reader to judge which particular plants he or she might prefer to seek. One of the joys of any auricula collection, however, is to see the wonderful contrast of the types and varieties unrolled along a greenhouse bench or standing next to each other in a frame. For this reason I have set out the plants in the list which follows in alphabetical order. A list of the plants within each category is given on pages 128 and 129.

I have made two exceptions to this rule. One is with the Stripes. Following the titanic achievement of Allan Hawkes in re-creating them, the work of developing them by Derek Parsons can never be underestimated. It is largely due to the efforts of these two men that the choice of plants available to us today is so broad. The explosion of colour and form to be found amongst the Parsons varieties is particularly noteworthy. I have, therefore, covered them as a small section on their own. The second addition to the main list is the breeding since 2000 of a new branch of Doubles by Derek Salt. Following his success with more mainstream types, Derek has begun to show us Striped Doubles of various colours but most noticeably with green pigment and tissue. These are not widely available and the breeder himself is commendably cautious about letting out plants which do not fulfil their early promise. I have shown a few of these after the Stripes in the hope that they will arouse the interest of more florists.

I describe some varieties which are currently agreed to be of the highest quality in circulation, others which are good and are readily available and the odd one which may be found but which is really quite ordinary. The number of good new introductions now appearing each year is encouraging but it means that any list may soon lose some of its validity. Please bear this in mind when using it. Any good nursery will tell you what is appearing at the national shows and, if they cannot, then you might be well advised to select another source of supply. Experienced growers may wonder why this or that plant is not included. The simple answer is that any list must have its limits and my apologies go to any who feel that their particular favourites have been ignored. It is also regrettable that while many plants bred in the Midlands and the north of England quickly find their way into circulation across all areas of the United Kingdom and abroad, those bred in the south of the country often enjoy a more local circulation. Any which you may come across but which do not appear in this list may still be beautiful and worthy of a place in your collection; it may just mean that they are amongst those which have not been let out to a wider public.

Ancient Society

April Moon

Ancient Society (Gold Centre Alpine) is one of the great introductions of recent years. Its form and colour are exemplars of what the Gold Centres are about. It is a reliable variety with few vices and puts up a stout stem topped by a full truss of half a dozen plus pips each of seven or eight nicely rounded petals. Older Gold Centres were plagued by wide tubes with a trumpet-like opening at the top. 'Ancient Society' shows a neat, round tube surrounded by a circular golden eye. This sets off the dark crimson at the base of each petal which then shades out through red to a pale orange at the periphery. The brightness of this colouring will bring a glow to anyone who catches sight of it, even on one of spring's duller days. At a time when many browns were becoming ever more sombre as a result of an overdose of 'Sirius' genes, 'Ancient Society' stood out as a reminder of the lighter side of the Gold Centres. The raiser, Ken Bowser, a President of the Northern Section of the National Auricula and Primula Society (N.A.P.S.), named the plant after the Ancient Society of York Florists who uphold florists'

standards across a wide range of plants. A practical tip from the raiser is not to overfeed 'Ancient Society'.

Andy Cole (Light Centre Alpine) is called after the football star who moved from Newcastle United to Manchester United in 1995, shortly after this plant was given its name, much to the chagrin of the breeder, Derek Telford. It is a sturdy grower with an equally sturdy habit of bloom. A truss of seven or eight pips is possible – an opulent sight. The tube is small and light, while the centre is never too wide, though its edge may not be most clearly delineated. The colour is a deep plum, shading out gently to a mid pink, though this may bear a little veining of the deeper colour. The pips are nicely rounded and generally quite flat.

Applecross (Gold Centre Alpine) – *see* 'Sandwood Bay'

April Moon (Yellow Self Show) was one of a group of Yellow Selfs introduced by Tim Coop from a cross between his own Yellow, 'Helen', and

Avril

David Hadfield's 'Moonglow'. This must rate as one of the most successful crosses ever, in that not only was 'April Moon' one of its progeny, but they also include other prizewinners such as 'Corntime', 'Sherbet Lemon', 'Moneymoon', 'Party Time', 'Lemon Drop' and 'Tomboy'. The plants vary in their shade of yellow from the solid and bright to the slightly more delicate. All are good plants but some may be inconsistent in their performance, not always coming up with the highest standard of pips and sometimes being just a little too vigorous. Should you have the opportunity to acquire one, however, seize it and give it some care, for they have all shown a will of their own when it comes to consistent performance. 'April Moon' shone on its first few appearances but then seemed to fade from the scene just a little before staging a resurgence. A

mature plant may sometimes rot off for no apparent reason, but as a rule it is a good doer and puts up a sturdy head of bright yellow pips above brightly mealed foliage.

Avril (Light Centre Alpine) is a vigorous plant which puts up a strong scape to support a nice head of bloom. The colour is a rich plum at the base, shading out to a pretty, paler edge. The tube and the eye are round and clear. Some attention may be needed if you want to exhibit your plant as it persists in throwing one pip on which two petals cockle (collide and stand up). It appears frequently among the prizewinners at national shows and is also simply a lovely thing to enjoy in the privacy of your own collection. The name comes from the wife of Ken Bowser who raised this plant.

Barbarella (Dark Self Show) was bred by Peter Ward using the pollen of the centenarian 'The Mikado'. The leaves carry a light dusting of meal which sets off admirably the very dark flowers. The plant can become lanky but is generally quite well behaved, producing adequate, though not abundant, offsets. Although no auricula can be accurately described as black, 'Barbarella' is of the very darkest shade of red. It is a colour which few auriculas approach and even fewer with the form of this plant. The golden tube and gleaming white paste set off the body colour beautifully. The only plant in general circulation which can match 'Barbarella' at the moment is 'The Mikado' and that is not such a reliable grower.

Beechen Green (Green Edge Show), bred by Lawrence Wigley, is a plant popular in the south but has never managed to find a foothold in the Midlands or the north. The edge is on the darker side of green and many carry speckles of farina.

Benny Green (Green Edge Show) is a recent introduction from Brian Coop, a former President of the Midlands Section of the N.A.P.S. and the breeder of many exciting new breaks in Self Coloured Show Auriculas. It is a stout grower with a real determination to provide the world with more stocks of itself, throwing numerous offsets round the collar. Removal can permit disease organisms to enter the plant where the offsets or buds are cut off, but they must be removed if the plant is to make a neat crown. When grown on that single crown, 'Benny Green' throws a strong stem which puts up a truss of five or more pips of the finest 1-3-6 proportions with a good coloured zone contrasting well with the fine paste and the well-rounded petals. A feature of these petals is that they are individually smaller than those in other leading varieties such as 'Jupiter' and 'Prague'. The breeder has succeeded, however, in giving us a bloom on which this does not lead to an interruption of the circularity of the periphery. 'Benny Green' is a young plant but one which looks like having a great future.

Barbarella

Benny Green

Bilbo Baggins

Bilbo Baggins (Gold Centre Alpine) is another of the truly splendid Alpines introduced in our new millennium. It came from John Radford, a Midlands member and a true character, who sadly died not long after giving this plant its perfectly formed blooms of beautiful form. The tube is neat and round with a bright, golden centre surrounding it. The colour starts out as a dark chestnut and shades out through a dark orange to a pale orange or peach at the edge. The pips are round and the petal texture luxurious. A head of bloom on a well-grown plant is a joy to behold. It is a plant of the highest quality.

Blossom (Gold Centre Alpine) is one of the older Alpines for which many growers still have a soft spot. Its golden centre sets off the silken black of the inner zone of colour which quickly shades out to the richest red. Caught on its day, it is a beautiful sight; but that day can be fleeting, for the black fades into an ashen colour recalling moiré silk. If you are looking for a more modern variety of this colouring, try 'Blyth Spirit' which follows later in this list.

Blue Chip (Fancy) gives a hint as to both the colour and the regard which Tim Coop had for this plant. It is still the one to beat in this shade, flaunting its deep blue body against a white edge. It even throws a sturdy truss of pips of a circular shape with a reasonably yellow tube and a good paste. A strong mature plant is a captivating sight, but 'Blue Chip', like a number of other Fancies of this persuasion, will often throw up autumn trusses, thus depriving the grower of the best flowers in the spring. It also likes to throw an unnecessarily large number of offsets which need to be culled if you hope to keep a strong main stem for good blooms. This is a variety to which I look forward every year.

Blue Cliff (Blue Self Show) is a relative newcomer and may not yet have settled down fully, but those who have found the knack of cultivating it enthuse about its qualities. It has a habit of leaning to one side and trying to produce a second main stem which does not aid any attempt to attain a neat shape to the crown. Its brightly mealed foliage, on the other hand, stands out clearly alongside many others and enhances its equally brightly coloured

Blossom

Blue Chip

Blue Cliff

blooms. These are not a true blue (the blue of the gentian does not exist in auriculas) and may even incline a little towards the slightly purple side, but a Blue Self this plant is. Both tube and paste are up with the best in the group and its vigour leaves little to be desired, for 'Blue Cliff' will put up a large head of pips which may need to be culled if each is to have room to itself without overlapping others nearby.

Blue Jean (Blue Self Show) is the earlier of two excellent Blues (see 'Oakes Blue') bred by Derek Telford and named as a compliment to his wife. When first introduced in 1973 it swept all other Blues before it. Now it often has to give way to more recent offerings, but it can still carry off prize cards at national shows. The plant stands out when not in bloom by virtue of its

Blue Steel

Blue Yodeler

rather long, pale green leaves which carry very little meal, a characteristic of very few Blues. The pips tend to be quite small and may even be shaded, but when the colour is solid they are as good as many others.

Blue Steel (Any Other Colour Self Show) originated in the greenhouse of Brian Coop and was the precursor of a number of very pale shades of blue, quite unlike anything which had been seen across the range of Show Auriculas. Its colour is largely conveyed by its name, being a steely or even icy blue. The colour of the truss is set off nicely by the lightly mealed foliage. It has its faults, such as a propensity to shade as the colour stretches towards the periphery of the pip and a sometimes fuzzy edge to the paste, but nevertheless it will always attract the eye when set amongst other auriculas. It has also served well as a parent at the head of several generations of seedlings of this type such as 'Watchet', 'Windermere' and 'Derwentwater'. All are remarkable for the delicacy and distinction of their colour and all are to be enjoyed either in the privacy of one's own garden or at any show, more especially the two latter varieties for Brian has now achieved what many had initially thought impossible, namely

the combination of a new colour and the classical form.

Blue Yodeler (Light Centre Alpine) and the Gold Centre 'Slim Whitfield' both take their names from singing stars of the mid-twentieth century. Both are rated highly by the florists and both are prominent amongst award-winning stands at the national shows. Their raiser, Ken Bowser, has given us a good number of auriculas of the highest standard and often with just a little difference from the majority of their kind. 'Blue Yodeler' is of this type. Tube and centre are neat, round and white, while the body begins as a good dark shade of mauve-blue which soon shades out to the palest version of the same, becoming almost white towards the periphery of the pip. The plant is a stout grower which puts up a handsome truss, well supported on strong pedicels, and provides the grower with a steady supply of offsets. Its only slight drawback is that it tends to bloom later than many Alpines, though this is a distinct advantage in an early season.

Blyth Spirit (Gold Centre Alpine) is one of a series of Alpine Auriculas bred by Dave Skinner who worked in the electricity generating

Blyth Spirit

industry and named his plants after power stations. For more than twenty years the flow of Gold Centres was dominated by the brown or orange side of the spectrum. For a number of years prior to that, red colours had predominated, especially the beautiful 'Blossom' (page 51), which was always inclined to throw odd faults but whose chief weakness lay in its greatest virtue, namely its rich, dark colour. This began near the eye as the darkest possible shade of red, amounting to black. The colour then ran out gradually into a rich, silken red at every edge. The problem was (and still is, if you can induce a plant of 'Blossom' to grow strongly) that the black zone was its opulent self for a very brief period before it developed an unbecoming grey sheen, rather like shot silk. This took away the freshness from the whole truss, especially when the blooms were only affected one by one. 'Blyth Spirit' has recaptured much of the essence of its predecessor but in a much lighter form. The dark zone is marginally less dark and less broad, while the outer parts of the petals are a very much brighter shade of red. Gone is any hint of tiredness and in its place is a wonderful freshness. The tube and eye are neat and well proportioned, as in nearly all of the most recent Gold Centre introductions. 'Blyth Spirit' is still a

new plant but, as the circulation becomes wider, get hold of one if you can.

Bob Lancashire (Green Edge Show) was bred by Jack Wemyss-Cooke in the 1980s. Originally quite promising, its form deteriorated and good pips are rarely seen today.

Bolero (Gold Centre Alpine) is an old plant from C.F. Hill of Birmingham who raised it in 1964. The name ending in 'o' is typical of those given by C.F. Hill and continued by Allan Hawkes who became a great companion of Mr. Hill and took up his breeding line after his friend's death. Although 'Bolero' never threw offsets with any freedom, it became an established favourite for many years and is still available today. The pips are well formed with a neat tube, a feature which not too many Gold Centres of its generation were able to display, and a good centre. The colour covers a very dark orange-red running out to a light coppery orange shade.

Brasso (Yellow Self Show) is yet another Yellow from Tim Coop but this time from a cross between 'Moonglow' and 'Upton Belle'. Unlike the 'April Moon' group, this plant is the sole representative of the pairing. It is a sturdy grower which provides adequate but not prolific offsets. It throws up a long main stem and puts up from this a good truss of solid yellow pips of good size and placement. It features regularly among the prizewinners at national shows.

Brimstone and Treacle (Double) is a story on its own which is told elsewhere in this book (page 22). Although I raised this auricula, it grew best for Ken Whorton, the great breeder and cultivator of Double Auriculas. Like a number of other Doubles it makes a dumpy plant with lightly mealed, slightly matt foliage from which springs a short scape. The truss is held aloft on short, stout pedicels. The pips are brown with stripes and streaks of yellow tissue and white farina. It is one of the few Striped Doubles. As an exhibition plant it has some

Brimstone and Treacle

faults: the brown colour intensifies as the pips age, so that the truss never consists of a uniform colour and it would be better if the scape were longer. The best example I have seen was more uniform and taller than I ever managed. It has the advantage for breeders that it produces viable pollen. So far, all its offspring have lacked any striping but they have been double in form. 'Brimstone and Treacle' is a sturdy plant with few vices and a definite will to grow and bloom.

Brompton (Yellow Self Show) was the pick of the Yellow Selfs for several years. In skilled hands, such as those of its breeder, David

Brasso

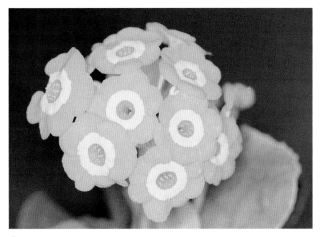

Brompton

55

Brookfield

Hadfield, it glowed with quality. The bright yellow petals have a solid texture with a good paste of the proper width and circularity of form. Despite the many assurances from the raiser, 'Brompton' proved more difficult in the hands of many growers. The vigour of the plants on the showbench was difficult to emulate and offsets were scarce, despite a plentiful supply from David to other growers. It has been suggested by those who have succeeded with 'Brompton' that this plant responds to a more than usually open compost to make sturdy root growth. Given the treatment which it prefers, it is a Yellow of real quality, the solid yellow blooms shining out against the well-powdered foliage.

Brookfield (White Edge Show) is a product of the breeding line which gave us 'Warwick' and 'Sharmans Cross'. It stands on the borderline between the Greys and the White Edges, just about falling into the White camp, while the other two usually tend in the opposite direction. It is certainly easier to grow than 'Warwick' and gives its offsets more liberally, but its trusses are not of the same quality. As with nearly every

White Edge, the pips are smaller than is customary in the Greys. The tube carries the odd crenation, though it is a good enough shade of gold. The paste is again a good width and texture, with the black body colour and the edge being just up to scratch. Its faults lie in the growth which tends to be lanky and the plant's habit of throwing one tiny, almost superfluous petal on some pips which stands out incongruously against the otherwise acceptable blooms. This failing has also been noted on some of its offspring, though it is not a feature which occurs on every pip. If 'Brookfield' were a little more squat in growth and just a tiny bit whiter in the edge, it would be a very good plant. Even so, it is a variety worth growing and can still win awards at national shows.

Buttermere (Double) was bred by Ken Whorton and was a beautiful replacement for the old, pale yellow 'Mary' which is discussed later in this list. Whereas the older variety refused to fill in the gap over the tube at the heart of each bloom, 'Buttermere' was classically formed. It has been seen at displays with as many as ten pips in a neat truss, each one leaving no hint of a fault. The full truss is backed nicely by matt green foliage. Unfortunately, the old fault of the open tube is reappearing as the plant ages and it is no longer quite as reliable as in its earlier days.

Buttermere

C.W. Needham (Light Centre Alpine) will not often be found on the showbench but it is still in many collections. Bred in 1934, it no longer has the most robust constitution in a pot, though you may be lucky and find it a suitable place in the garden border. It is one of a small number of 'blue' Light Centres which date from the first half of the twentieth century and which enjoyed great popularity as exhibition varieties right through the 1980s. The tube is a neat circle and the eye is light, though it often comes angular. The pips shade from dark to light violet-blue and may not always be flat. The blue also varies from season to season according to ambient light and temperature; they may even vary from one pip to another on the same truss. Blues are often prone to this.

Cameo Beauty (Double) possesses a haunting beauty. It is well named for its blooms have all the appearance of an old cameo brooch. Its beauty comes at a price for it is not amongst the easiest to grow and has to be sought out. The pips are beautifully formed and open a pale shade of cream with a buff to brown centre, the opposite configuration from the jewellery. The colours change as the pips mature, which means that the variety is at a potential disadvantage on the showbench since the judges will prefer pips which each display the same (or nearly the same) colour. Despite this, seek out the plant and look carefully at its form and charm. You may find yourself captivated too.

Chanel, **Chiffon** and **Taffeta** (Any Other Colour Self Show) are, all three, delicate shades of lavender pink bred by Tim Coop. 'Taffeta' is widely grown and is a sturdy plant. 'Chiffon' is slightly more difficult to cultivate successfully. 'Chanel' is not met with as frequently as the other two but has appeared more often amongst the prizewinners at national shows. They are nicely mealed and look quite pleasing when not in bloom. The tube and paste on each one is good and the pip generally round though the odd notch may occur, as it does with many Selfs. This failing seems to affect 'Taffeta' more than the other two. Their main fault when they appear at shows is that the colour shades out from the paste to the edge. Such shading, however gentle, will not find favour in the eyes of a judge, but most of us will cherish any of these in the privacy of our own garden and just enjoy their delicacy and their note of difference from their fellows.

C.W. Needham

Taffeta

Cheyenne (Red Self Show) is one of a group of Red Selfs bred by Peter Ward and named after American native tribes or, in one case, after a particular leader, 'Geronimo'. 'Kiowa' is the other member of the clan which is found either offered for sale or on the showbench. All are derived from an older plant with good form and not too much brightness in its colouring. Peter's aim was to add the good form of this variety to the colour of some of the existing Reds. He went quite a long way towards achieving his goal. The form of his introductions was superior to the older types but the colours, even though genuine Reds, did

Cheyenne

not display the brilliance for which he had hoped. Nevertheless, all three plants still achieve awards at the shows and provide the grower with a satisfying plant to enjoy in a frame, greenhouse or (given a spell of dry weather) in the open border, for these are real toughies. They have few idiosyncrasies and show a determination to live and to reproduce. The yellow cast to the farina on their leaves in the winter and early spring is a little odd to some eyes and very attractive to others, but it makes the plants easy to spot amongst many others.

Chiquita (Double) is another of Ken Whorton's superb introductions. The lay of the bloom resembles that of many old roses with its curled inner petals and rounded outline. The colour is a rich cinnamon brown at the heart with a charming border of a paler shade of rusty orange round the rim of each petal. The foliage is a bright shade of green and the whole plant makes a picture of extrovert verve. It is encountered frequently amongst the award winners at shows.

Chloë (Green Edge Show) remains an enduring enigma. When I first started growing auriculas in the 1970s it was fabled and scarce. It has never become plentiful and even a tiny offset is a

Chiquita

Chloë

Clare

precious acquisition. Once potted and in a safe place under cover, persuading it to thrive and bloom is just as difficult and yet a small number of the very best growers seem to accomplish this feat most springs. Its raiser, Fred Buckley, was a noted grower of the mid-twentieth century who was reputed to have used a number of old varieties in his breeding programme. Buckley was never known for generosity with his plants and it was not until after his death, when Dr. Duncan Duthie purchased the collection and began to make the plants available, that 'Chloë' and her kindred came into the hands of a greater number of cultivators. The periphery of the pips is notably smooth and circular. The body colour is none too wide and a good black, though it reddens as the pip ages. The paste is solid, round and shining white, but its main attraction lies in the form of its golden tube (as does that of many another Green Edge). The top of the tube is circular but narrows just below the anthers to form a neat, shallow cup, the fabled 'Buckley' tube. The effect of the shape is to preclude any glimpse of the shadowy, lower end at the base, thus focusing the eye on the concentric circles which constitute the bloom. On those pips without any of the double-sized (bull-nosed) petals which occur on many edged varieties, the effect is magical, a scintilla of perfection.

'Chloë' has never been an easy plant to cultivate. Some well-known growers have complained of the difficulty of keeping it alive and vigorous; others say that it makes strong growth but puts up only two or three pips. Occasionally one comes across those who have the knack of producing superb specimens. Their methods vary from a very open growing medium of 50% soil-based compost and 50% grit to a more substantial mix of soil-based and multi-purpose compost with a good measure of grit. The feeding regime also varies from little and often to two mild splashes of feed in a year. If anyone ever manages to provide a constant formula for success, all growers of Green Edges will be grateful. In the meantime, the riddle persists.

Clare (Grey Edge Show) is a plant bred by Peter Ward from a cross between 'Walhampton' and 'Helena'. It is a stout grower but tends to climb upwards into a palm-tree shape and can die off as a result. It is, however, a reliable flowerer and sets seed without too much difficulty. The edge is a mid-grey with a pleasing black ground and nice paste. The tube is the weakness with this variety for it follows many of the older Grey Edges in its over-large width and its crenated rim. A large pip may lose the elegance of the very best varieties. 'Walhampton', the seed parent, was much neater, though its body was too narrow. The pollen parent is not a plant which one can recommend nowadays and is probably the main cause of 'Clare's' undistinguished tube.

Coffee (Fancy) originates from the same cross ('Lovebird' x 'Teem') that gave us 'Margaret Martin'. To the best of my knowledge, Gwen Baker, the hybridist and one of the great figures of the primula and auricula world in the second half of the twentieth century, did not succeed in coming up with a black-ground Grey of any note from the resulting seedlings, but presented instead a plant which enthused and inspired many a grower and hybridist. 'Coffee' has the same crenated and often wide tube as

Conservative

'Lovebird', but the paste and edge can be of good quality, despite some frilliness of the pip and, nowadays, some pointed petals. But it is the body colour which was such a break in the 1970s. Fancies then tended to carry a yellow ground with some having instead a zone of purple, mauve or red. 'Coffee' lived up to its name. Peter Ward and Gwen herself described it in their book as café au lait, a description which needs no further elaboration. In its heyday 'Coffee' was a tall grower with long, strong stems and splendid overall vigour. More recently it has shown signs of age but it retains a distinction of hue which nothing has surpassed.

Conservative (Fancy) is an enigma. It was purchased at a Northern Section plant sale by David Hadfield who persuaded it to make a sturdy plant. When shown in prime form, it is a variety that never fails to halt passers-by in their steps. At the centre of its blooms is a bright, golden tube of perfect neatness and circularity. This is surrounded by a broad, gleaming white paste beyond which is a fierce red body, contrasting superbly with the dense white meal towards the edge. Unfortunately, 'Conservative' does not adhere strictly to the form of either the edged or the striped types,

forming an edge from which white farina feathers down towards the paste. The arresting contrast between the red and the white remains of the brightest, despite its presumed age, for the House of Douglas offered a plant of this name for sale in the 1960s, though that variety had a black ground. Both forms are in circulation and it is said that the black-ground White Edge will throw the red/white form, if grown strongly. The colouring came out in striped seedlings bred by Allan Hawkes, after he had used pollen from 'Conservative' provided by David Hadfield. It is not an easy plant to cultivate, being a sickly grower with stunted, yellow-blotched foliage and a proclivity for rotting off at the collar. A bright specimen is rare but worth all the trouble.

Corntime (Yellow Self Show) is a member of the 'April Moon' tribe of Yellow Selfs which has faded and re-emerged. The blooms are not quite of the calibre of 'April Moon' but it is a sturdy grower and has won a Premier award.

Corporal Jones and **Sergeant Wilson** (Grey Edge Show) were both grey-haired figures in the popular British *Dad's Army* television series, so it comes as no surprise to find their names attached to grey-edged auriculas. Both showed good form on their first outings into the wide world but later tended to produce fewer and smaller pips, while at the same time developing an untidy, lanky habit. Although the raiser, Bob Taylor, despaired of them and advised consigning them to the compost heap, one or two determined individuals still manage to induce them to produce some reasonable blooms and they both continue to appear at the shows.

Corrie Files (Double) was bred by Cliff Timpson who astounded all the breeders of auriculas when he revealed that it was a seedling of the Gold Centre Alpine, 'Sirius' which has no other hint of doubling in its make-up. 'Corrie

Files' carries a bright red, fully double bloom and makes a mark amongst some of the paler shades that may occur in the Doubles.

Crimple (Fancy) is one of two extraordinary plants (the other being 'Crinoline') which Tim Coop gave to the world in the late 1990s. It flowers early and so may be seen at the shows in years when spring comes late, but it appears in growers' collections everywhere, for there is nothing like it except its children and they look very similar to the parent but without its magical quality. It has a habit of setting a tight truss of buds at the base of the foliage some time during late autumn which persist through the winter as a reminder of the good things to come when the weather finally brightens and the slightest hint of spring warmth begins to encourage new growth. Indeed, it is worth keeping a plant or two somewhere to the fore in your collection just as a little encouragement that winter is nearly over and that, despite a few frosts to come, a new season is on the way. From its green foliage, the plant sends up a strong stem which carries a good-sized truss of green-edged pips with a nice tube, smooth, round paste and a striking pale violet body. The body colour may fade a little as the pips age, but it contrasts

Crimson Glow

beautifully with the light green of the edge. The petals may be slightly pointed and other odd faults may appear, but they cannot detract from the striking balance of the body colour and the green edge. The plant has few vices. It grows neatly and sturdily, whilst providing a good supply of offsets.

Crimson Glow (Double) is a plant which seems to shout out to all those who are attracted to Doubles. It lives up to its name with fiery crimson, slightly open blooms, permitting just a glimpse of the underlying yellow at the heart of the pips. It is thought by a number of those who are familiar with it to be losing some of its early vigour, yet despite this handsome examples can be seen at shows, both competitive and non-competitive. If you want a Double to blaze out amongst your collection, 'Crimson Glow' might be a good place to start.

Crinoline (Fancy) is another Tim Coop raising which catches the eye as very different from the majority of auriculas, but provides a challenge to write an adequate description of its blooms. It also provides something of a challenge to the grower for it has a very lax habit of growth,

Crimple

Crinoline

sending out a long main stem that bends over across the top of the pot and from which odd shoots emerge to provide a small number of new offsets. It does not take kindly to discipline, but a few experts have been known to persuade 'Crinoline' to retain a reasonably acceptable shape. Flower scapes may also try to elongate more than one might wish but when a well-shaped plant provides a well-formed scape and truss, the whole thing is a sight to admire. The blooms are a confection of green, grey, and mauve, not quite an Edge, not quite a Stripe and breathtakingly beautiful. The tube is quite nice and the paste as bright as anyone might wish. When exhibited (or just grown in your own frame or greenhouse) in its best form, this plant will cause any viewer to pause, admire and enthuse.

Denim (Fancy) is a young plant of limited availability but shows all the signs of being a variety which many will want to acquire. It is very different from any Fancy which has gone before. The raiser, Terry Atkinson, a former President of the Northern Section of the N.A.P.S., deployed an enormous amount of knowledge, insight and vision in its genesis. The plant forms a tight crown of lightly mealed leaves from which a strong stem arises. The truss of six or so pips is held on firm footstalks. The pips have the usual paler tube of the blue shades with a clean, white, round paste. The blue body is of the pale hue aptly described by the name but fades suddenly close to the periphery to the very palest version of sky blue, leaving what looks for all the world

Denim

like a laced Self Show Auricula. It is a unique variation and one can only hope that further breeding might throw even more blooms of a comparable format. Should you ever be in a position to beg or borrow an offset, seize it immediately.

Dilly Dilly (Light Centre Alpine) was aptly named by Keith Leeming who reminded those present at its first introduction in public of the song 'Lavender's blue dilly dilly'. It is one of the very best of the blue Light Centres. It is also a tricky thing to maintain in a sturdy condition. It offsets adequately but also rots easily and sometimes refuses to thrive when other varieties that have received identical treatment are in the rudest health. A well-grown, sturdy plant in bloom, however, is the epitome of delicacy. The tube is small and round, the centre is very pale and circular, while the colouring starts from a narrow band of very deep violet and shades out into a broader zone of pale lavender which is remarkably solid and yet appears almost translucent. The very broadness of this outer colour, combined with the pale underlying tissue, lends the whole truss an air of innocence

and refinement which contrast well with many of the more boisterous shades to be found amongst the Alpines. The pips are firmly supported on strong footstalks and look up into the face of the spectator. This is a real treasure and one to tackle, if you can find a plant.

Divint Dunch (Light Centre Alpine) is a decent Light Centre which owes its name to the north-east of England, home of its raiser, Derek Telford. In the local version of English it comes out as 'Don't knock us' or 'Don't touch'. The plant grows without difficulty and sends up nice heads of bluish plum-coloured flowers. The tube is neat and the eye small but it may not be totally smooth in its outline. The seven or eight petals making up the pip are of a good texture and have a smooth periphery.

Douglas White (White Edge Show) is one of many nice White Edges supplied by The House of Douglas in the twentieth century. Common to many was a small, neat, round waxy, golden tube. The black grounds could be narrow and carry meal, while the outline of the pips was not always circular, but the farina of the edge was always dense. Two plants from the strain were acquired by Dr.

Dilly Dilly

Duncan Duthie who distributed them to other breeders in the hope of increasing the number of available Whites. The better one of this pair is known as 'Douglas White 4x'. The last proprietor of the Edenside Nurseries, Gordon Douglas, rated his seedlings by number, the higher the better. This particular one obviously stood quite high in his esteem.

Doyen (Double) was bred in 1982 by Gwen Baker, a prominent member of the Midlands and West Section of the N.A.P.S. and co-author with Peter Ward of an earlier book on auriculas. It is a deep red with a hint of gold at the base of each petal. Initially a vigorous grower, it has now lost some of its energy and is less frequently seen at the shows. More recent introductions have a less informal lay to the petals. It remains, however, a handsome plant with a glowing truss of pips and no untoward habits in its culture.

Eaton Dawn (Any Other Colour Self Show) is yet another superb example of the huge debt we owe Brian Coop for his vision and persistence in seeking to extend the range of colours available to all growers. After several quite reasonable plants, Brian produced one of real quality and persistence in 'Eaton Dawn'. Its colour of a lilac pink is solid across the broad petals, whose texture

Eaton Dawn

leaves nothing to be desired. The tube is round and smooth, surrounded by a broad paste to give the traditional 1-3-6 proportions to the pip. The light green foliage completes a picture of delicacy and distinction. If you should find this or the later and very similar variety 'Miss Otis', grab either or preferably both. They are excellent.

Fairy Moon (Fancy) – *see* 'Moon Fairy'

Fanfare (Fancy) is a bold mixture which presents a challenge to both the skill and the patience of the grower. It carries a shining white edge enclosing a striking, red body that may not be circular but which attracts the attention as soon as one approaches the plant. The paste is solid and white while the tube is a waxen yellow with a slightly raised rim to enhance its circularity. When well grown, it is a sight to remember. The difficulty is to persuade 'Fanfare' to produce such a plant. It grows away strongly but too often wants to split its main stem into two branches. If this is allowed to proceed, it leads to a weakening of both stems with small trusses of poor blooms. Unfortunately, the removal of one of the two arms may lead to rot at the point where it was removed or to the production of a plethora of side buds further down which may again weaken the main stem. The plant may also throw its nicely mealed leaves without putting too much effort into flowering. Despite all this, 'Fanfare' throws a good number of strong offsets which allows the grower the opportunity to induce one to develop into a sturdy plant that will put up its strong stem with a healthy truss of five or six pips. The sight of such a plant (and possibly the 'oohs' and 'aahs' of all who see it) are sufficient reward for the effort.

Figaro (Green Edge Show) is one of the best Green Edges of modern times. Its name gives a hint as to its breeder, for David Hadfield, whose record in producing numerous Show

Fanfare

Figaro

Auriculas of the highest quality can only be matched by names such as Ben Simonite, one of the original members of the National Auricula Society in 1876, has a taste for the music of Mozart. Varieties include names such as 'Haffner', 'Jupiter', 'Paris', 'Prague' and 'Tamino', all having a connection with either a symphony or an opera by that great composer. 'Figaro' ranks among the best. It was the result of a line of breeding which began with 'Chloë' and 'Fleminghouse' and, even though David occasionally brought other varieties into his breeding programme, many of those which were to become well known drew their genes chiefly from these two. The parentage of 'Figaro' is given as 'Chloë' x 'Haffner', while 'Haffner' is shown as a 'Fleminghouse' cross. The main feature of the plant is its vigour. It grows without too much difficulty and throws up its trusses of bloom with impressive regularity. Its offsets appear in good numbers, without sapping too much energy from the parent plant, and root without any great problems. It is the only

Green Edge which has grown in my garden border, though any rain immediately destroyed the paste. For all of these reasons it is one of the most widely grown and shown Green Edges of modern times and an excellent Green for the new enthusiast. The pips themselves have a smooth, circular, bright, golden tube, the anthers being set off by the cup which lies directly below them. The paste is solid, dense and white and the body is of a good width with the requisite dark colouring feathering out finely into the bright green edge. The whole pip is more towards the old 1-3-6 proportions found in many Grey Edges than the 1-2-4 so often seen in the Greens. If you have room for just one Green Edge, this is the one to select.

Finchfield (Gold Centre Alpine) is named after an area of Wolverhampton by its raiser, Gwen Baker, who lived in that part of the city. It was one of a number of similar plants which she introduced in the mid- to late 1970s and which were eagerly sought by the growers of the time who had access to more bright reds than to the striking browns of this group. The two other winners from the same cross are 'Goldthorn' and 'Merridale', also named after parts of Wolverhampton. 'Finchfield' remained the most popular of the three because the other two produced either too few offsets or were so prolific around the collar that it was difficult to find a plant with a sturdy central crown to carry a good truss of bloom. 'Finchfield' also has a tendency to over-offset, needing a firm hand to focus its mind on making the best of its rich colouring. This is a good, dark brown which shades out to a lighter orange.

Fleminghouse (Green Edge Show) came from the Pennines and long remained a plant of the north of England. It constituted a challenge to 'Chloë' amongst the growers of Cheshire, Lancashire and Yorkshire during the 1970s and '80s but failed to find a following elsewhere. It was one of those plants which seemed to take a delight in the cooler climate of the hills, refusing to do well further south. Today its early vigour has gone and its form cannot be compared with that of more modern raisings, despite the fact that it played an important role in the first generations of seedlings from raisers such as

Fleminghouse

David Hadfield. Its weaknesses for show purposes at present are its crenated tube and its tendency to come with a China Edge. In the 1980s these faults were not so apparent and photographs show a fine, highly attractive Green. Its proportions are a good 1-3-6 with a nice, black body and solid paste. If you can persuade 'Fleminghouse' to prosper you may be rewarded with a glimpse of its splendid past.

Frank Crosland (Light Centre Alpine) is another old-timer amongst the Blues. Like 'C.W. Needham' it was raised in Cheshire but four years earlier, in 1930. The pips are striking, often larger and fewer in number than many Alpines. Should you find yourself confronted by a plentiful truss, you may be disappointed by the results. This is definitely a plant where less is better. The tube is neat, though sometimes a little oval (a deft but gentle rolling between the forefinger and thumb shortly prior to staging may alleviate this), and the eye, though it may show the odd irregularity where the petals join, is generally circular. The colour starts as a dark blue adjacent to the eye but quickly blends into a broader zone of mid-blue with an ever paler version of the same right at the edge. The whole pip projects a simple elegance. 'Frank Crosland' featured in many award-winning exhibits up to the 1980s but mainly in the hands of northern growers. It is one of a number of plants which were reputed to have geographical preferences. It can also be quite idiosyncratic, allowing a stock of sturdy plants to be built up only for them all to rot off within a couple of years of each other.

Fred Booley (Double) is a fine lilac-blue double, able to put up strong trusses of ten or even more pips. The colour is very much after the fashion of some recent so-called 'blue' roses but its habit is much more vigorous than those. The pips have a round row of guard petals at the back that remain cupped for a while but then open out flat, nicely

Fred Booley

Galatea

Funny Valentine

framing the fullness of the centre which is almost imbricated (like the tiles on a Roman roof) in its lay. This is another variety much employed by leading exhibitors and available through several commercial sources.

Funny Valentine (Double) looks for all the world like a gallica rose. Not only are the blooms a similar shade of deep, rich purple, they also form cups as they emerge from the buds, though these later flatten out more and lighten in shade, revealing a hint of yellow at the base. Since it was first introduced by Ed Picken and his daughter, Laura, this has been

a constant success amongst the growers and is widely available. It has character and opulence without too many difficulties and is a good plant for your collection.

Galatea (Grey Edge Show) is not quite of the standard of 'Grey Hawk', but, being from the same breeder, there can be little doubt as to its quality. It grows without too many demands and produces just enough offsets to maintain a stock. Its leaves are nicely mealed and densely produced where the carrot rises from the compost serving to cover the top of the pot as demanded by the criteria of old. The tube is slightly crenated but a bright shade of yellow with just enough of a cup below the anthers to leave no dark area visible beneath. The paste is a fine white, though the petal edges may just cut into it a little. When this occurs, it loses the round outer edge of the very best. The body is a narrow band of black with fine feathering. Its narrowness may sometimes mean that it all but disappears or carries a few flecks of meal which may not disconcert the eye in the privacy of one's own garden but which a show judge may not regard too highly. The edge itself is a light shade of grey, deriving, no doubt, from paler underlying tissue which is lightly speckled with farina. If you have the opportunity to obtain a little piece of this variety, seize it, for it is better than many of the older stalwarts and has the advantage of youth on its side. A glance at the results of national shows will reveal that 'Galatea' has won a number of awards, both as a single plant and as a member of multi-pot groups. An interesting feature of this plant is its name. When asked whether with 'Galatea' David Hadfield had abandoned Mozart in favour of Handel, the breeder replied that it came from a battleship.

Gary Pallister (Gold Centre Alpine) is a variable plant which may appear bright but not garish or, on a bad day, a little too dark. It

Gavin Ward

is quite a good grower and throws up a nice truss of half a dozen pips. The tube and eye are a good gold and the colour runs from very dark red to a brown-orange. When this is fresh it looks quite distinguished, but beware the duller shades which may be present on a bad day. Despite that, the variety is popular with exhibitors and is frequently found in award-winning exhibits.

Gavin Ward (Grey Edge Show) is undoubtedly the most difficult of the Ward Greys to cultivate successfully, even more problematical than 'Warwick'. For this reason it is rarely seen on the showbench but, when it does deign to make itself available for display, it is worth the wait and the grower's effort. A testimony to the breeder's estimation of the plant is the fact that he named it after his son. The tube is round and yellow with just the slightest crenation, the paste is white and solid and the body colour a nice, dark black of a pleasing width with very fine

Gary Pallister

feathering. The edge is of a bright shade with an even coating of fine farina. The evenness of the petals is a feature of the plant, lending the whole truss a refined look. The neatness of the 1-3-6 proportions draws the eye as one stands near a group of plants containing this variety. A fully flattened truss of five pips is a gratifying sight. Grab an offset, if you are so fortunate, and care for it well.

Gay Crusader (Gold Centre Alpine) came from Les Kaye who took its name from a Derby winner, a tactic he employed on several occasions. Despite dating back to 1982, 'Gay Crusader' has continued to win awards at national shows. It is a dark red shading out to a peachy red at the periphery.

Geronimo (Red Self Show) – *see* 'Cheyenne'

Gizabroon (Dark Self Show) – *see* 'Super Para'

Godfrey (White Edge Show) is an exemplary White Edge, bearing testimony

Godfrey

to the skill and the good eye of its raiser, Bob Taylor, the long-time Editor and Secretary of the Northern Section of the N.A.P.S. It still exists in very limited numbers but, on its rare forays into public view, it shows a genuinely white edge, good strong black body with fine feathering, solid white paste and smooth golden tube. If this plant should ever be offered, accept it gratefully. Its name comes from the lovable, equally white-haired character in the old British television series, *Dad's Army*. If 'Godfrey' can ever be persuaded to bulk up and permit a wider spread, it could be amongst the best.

Golden Hind (Double) is less full than many varieties but has a colouring which is impossible to walk past. It looks very similar to a French marigold with a red base to each petal and an outer zone of a peachy yellow. This is another plant which crops up less frequently than earlier at the shows, as it has lost some of its youthful vigour, but is such a bright sight in one's own collection that it is worth a place.

Gordon Douglas (Light Centre Alpine) was raised by James Douglas of Great Bookham in 1918. It is a deeper shade of blue than 'C.W. Needham' and 'Frank Crosland', both of which date from the early part of the twentieth century. Glimpsed from a distance, it draws the eye with its dramatic colouring which shades less than in the two other varieties. Seen from close up, it often displays a number of faults. The eye can be noticeably cream and is frequently angular. In its prime it could throw trusses of numerous pips which needed judicious culling and manipulation to produce quality blooms. Its vigour has waxed and waned; some vigour was restored after the plant was micro-propagated, but it appears to have suffered a relapse.

Green Café

Green Café (Fancy) has won a number of prize cards without being of the highest quality. It is one of a small group of green-edged brown-bodied plants which came out of some early experiments with crosses between Standard Show Auriculas and plants with (at that time) non-acceptable body colours. The tube is reasonably yellow, though not of the brightest, but shows some crenation. The paste is a good white ring, while the green edge can be on the dull side. The body is a foxy brown and flashes up the petal edges, thus leaving the green edge at times almost heart-shaped. Despite what sounds like a total condemnation, 'Green Café' can produce seedlings of a similar and sometimes deeper hue. One problem with colouring of this type (in Self Show Auriculas as well as in this group) is a tendency for the body colour to shade out to a lighter version as it spreads away from the paste and this manifests itself all too frequently in the offspring. Nevertheless, 'Green Café' forms one starting point for other edged varieties with this type of ground colour. 'Green Mustard', 'Snuff' and 'Miss Teak' are similar plants in varying shades of brown.

Grey Hawk (Grey Edge Show) is another plant from David Hadfield, to whom we owe so many Green Edges. It results from a cross between a grey-edged, yellow-ground Fancy and the white-edged, maroon-ground Fancy, 'Hawkwood'. Both plants were chosen for various aspects of their form. In the case of 'Hawkwood', the quality sought was its exemplary, neat, golden, smooth-edged tube. Not only was David successful in achieving this, he also produced the solid black colour body missing in both of the parents. Most of the leading Greys prior to the introduction of 'Grey Hawk' display a crenated tube which, should it be at all pronounced, can detract from the overall circularity of the bloom. With 'Grey Hawk' this fault was eliminated. Its round tube stands out at the centre of a 1-3-6 pip. The quality of the paste is of the highest, while the body is of a good black, somewhat broader than had previously become customary and reminiscent of those varieties beloved of the growers of the nineteenth and early twentieth centuries. The final distinguishing feature of this plant is the particular combination of the meal and its underlying tissue on the edge. This tissue is essentially the green material of a leaf. This density and the size of the

Grey Hawk

individual specks of farina give the individual shades of grey. If the leaf tissue is light green and the scattering of the farina is reasonably light, something akin to peppermint green ensues. If the tissue is a very dark shade of green, the same meal can provide a heavy sombre effect. 'Grey Hawk' is neither. When the plant was first put on the showbench in 1989 I wrote that it had 'the leaden look, beloved of the growers of earlier generations'. This phrase has been repeated by other writers since then, but I still have no other description to characterise 'Grey Hawk'. Its tissue is a dull but not sombre green, while the farina is fine and evenly scattered, lending the whole pip an air of quiet refinement. Initially, 'Grey Hawk' was an easy plant to cultivate with great energy and even a tendency to split into two crowns, both of which could carry trusses of show standard. After that 'first, fine, careless rapture' 'Grey Hawk' has not been so free with either growth or blooms of the highest quality. Growers complain that it will not send up sturdy shoots or plentiful trusses. Varieties do come and go and some even stage resurgences. If you can persuade this one to grow strongly, you will not be disappointed. It is a truly beautiful sight.

Grüner Veltliner (Green Edge Show) From the same cross as 'Moselle', this plant is a little

Grüner Veltliner

Hawkwood

more temperamental and has a tendency to rot off. If you can master it (and that feat is achieved by florists in the north-east of England), it is worth growing.

Haffner (Green Edge Show) is another Mozartian memento from a breeding line involving 'Fleminghouse'. It does not have a reputation for reliable show trusses but still puts up slightly darker green blooms than most. The tube is a variable feature with a little too much irregularity in its outline. Despite these criticisms, a number of growers in the north-east of England have been successful on the showbench in recent years with very acceptable plants of 'Haffner'.

Hawkwood (Fancy) is an old plant from the House of Douglas. It is a light Grey Edge with a striking maroon-red body. This stands out against not only the finely mealed edge but also against the brilliant, smooth whiteness of the paste. The pips will flatten reasonably well on a good plant but too often insist on remaining cup-shaped. This is a huge pity as its tube is exemplary, being neat, round, smooth, golden and well-filled with anthers. The tube was a feature which caught the eye of that great breeder, David Hadfield, who used 'Hawkwood' as the pollen parent of 'Grey Hawk'. Constant vigilance is needed to restrict 'Hawkwood' to a single crown, for a plethora of offsets round the collar detracts from the vigour of the main stem and therefore from the form of the pips arising from it. Beware too that the cup-shaped pips can be passed on to any offspring. If you are seeking a willing grower amongst the Fancies, however, try 'Hawkwood'.

Hew Dalrymple (Green Edge Show) is one of the few remaining plants raised by C.G. Haysom at the Bartley Nurseries in the New Forest (Hampshire) in the years immediately after the Second World War. It boasts a bright emerald green to its edge and a round, golden tube. The paste is a good white but it flashes out into little peaks rather than keeping to the requisite circular shape while the black body colour, which suffers as a result, is very narrow. And yet it is the narrowness of the body together with the distinctive colour of its green which has attracted growers and raisers. It was one of the parents of Bob Taylor's 'Moselle' and 'Grüner Veltliner', used to counteract the heavier body of the other parent, 'Orb'.

Highland Park (Light Centre Alpine) is a pretty plant. It is regularly seen on the showbench and seems to live happily without problems. The eye may be a little on the small side but is generally acceptable for show purposes. It may, however, carry the odd fleck of meal which would bring about a disqualification at a show. The colour is a good violet shading out to a pale lilac pink.

Hinton Fields (Fancy) is a Green Edge with a yellow ground, much after the fashion of 'Sweet Pastures'. The body is too broad for the plant to be considered a serious show variety but it stands out nicely in the Fancy classes or set amongst more staid colours in one's private collection. It was bred by C.G. Haysom, a nurseryman of the 1940s and '50s, and carries the name of a village in Hampshire, as did many a variety that came from the Bartley Nurseries. The edge is a little more sombre than the green of 'Spring Meadows' and a well-grown plant is needed before the pips will grow with any degree of flatness, but, when they do, the cultivator will also be rewarded with a splendidly round tube, a feature all too easily overlooked by those who decry the Fancies without too close an examination. This tube may be passed on to its progeny, but so is the yellow body which can prove dominant in successive generations. One characteristic I discovered amongst the second and third generations from a 'Hinton Fields' x 'Chloë' cross is the appearance of brown body colours. The combination of green edge and brown body appeals to some, but not to others. Unfortunately all the plants I have produced have lacked a nice regular ring of colour and the brown has also shown a propensity to shade out from the paste towards the edge. A more persistent breeder may have greater success. 'Hinton Fields' has been micro-propagated and is readily available from the specialist nurseries and even from some garden centres.

Hot Lips

Hot Lips (Fancy) is another scarce variety which one hopes might become more widely cultivated. It arose amongst a batch of striped seedlings raised by Derek Parsons, the man who has given the world the vast majority of current Stripes. Its provenance is plain to see. From the lightly mealed leaves springs a strong stem that carries a slightly open truss of about half a dozen pips. The tube is small and golden but very crenated. The paste is very narrow with a fuzzy edge, but beyond this lies the chief attraction of this variety, the dusky salmon-pink of the body, liberally and evenly sprinkled with dots of fine meal. The whole truss looks as though it has just been dusted with icing sugar. A close inspection may also reveal indications of stripes amidst the powdering. Seedlings of this type are exceedingly rare and, despite raising many thousands of new plants over a number of years, Derek says that he has never found a comparable one amongst them. Unfortunately, 'Hot Lips' is not the easiest variety to cultivate. A sturdy specimen may rot off when it appears in rude health and offsets are thrown only in moderation. We can but hope that this one will change its mind and persist so that a wider public may enjoy its almost unique looks.

Iago (Grey Edge Show) is one of two seedlings from a 'Grey Friar' x 'Stephen' cross made by David Hadfield and shown in 1988. The raiser did not consider this to be one of his better efforts, but it still appears at the national shows. The tube is a lightish yellow and smoother in outline than some, though not as strikingly circular as in 'Grey Hawk'. The paste is of good quality, though there may be a hint of fuzziness at its outer edge. The body colour is a solid black and pleasingly broad enough to make its presence felt. It has a tendency, however, to flash markedly up the edge of the petals and sometimes allows the light grey edge to peak down at the centre of the pip until it all but touches the paste. The

Iago

Ian Greville

petals too lack a certain regularity in shape and size which may lend an air of untidiness to the pips. To add to the plant's odd character, the edge may sometimes come light enough for the exhibitor to wonder whether this plant actually belongs amongst the White Edges. All in all this is not in the highest rank, but is still a variety which wins awards on the showbench.

Ian Greville (Light Centre Alpine), bred by Cliff Timpson, is a favourite amongst the exhibitors and rightly so. It figures very frequently amongst prizewinning exhibits. It catches the attention of the spectator with its light pink aspect. A closer inspection will reveal that this is suffused almost strawberry-pink and covers quite a wide area of the pip. The colour at the base is a much darker shade of rosy crimson. The centre and the tube are also light, bright, exceptionally round and of neat proportions. This is a handsome plant but not one which takes readily to building up into a stout specimen. Even experienced growers have been heard to complain about its problematical nature. Once glimpsed at a show, however, it is worthwhile trying your hand with this one.

Jac (Blue Self) was given to the author by the raiser, Steve Popple, in 2007. Its first flowering was very encouraging. The truss was made up of five pips, each of a solid, deep blue without any hint of the shading found on so many Blue Selfs. The pure white paste stood out in striking contrast with a neat small tube at the centre. The blooms are backed by pleasantly mealed foliage. Steve's estimation of the plant is demonstrated by the fact that he named it after his daughter.

Jack Wood (Green Edge Show) was raised by David Hadfield and named after a *Garden News* journalist. On its initial appearances it was very promising and occasional handsome plants may still be seen, but it was never an easy plant to grow and to build up a stock with, so it is rarely seen nowadays.

James Arnot (White Edge Show) was another raising of Tom Meek, a long-time editor of the Northern Section and writer of articles under the pseudonym of Teem, the name he bestowed on his best-known seedling. It has a good, golden tube and solid paste, though the black body is on the narrow side. Its white-edged petals are often notched, thus spoiling the circular outline which a good pip should have. It is, however, a genuine White.

Jane Myers (Double) was one of the most popular Doubles of its time when it was bred by

Joel

Len Bailey in 1976. The pips are less full and geometrical in their lay than more modern types but the cream-coloured petals still manage to cover over the tube at the centre. Although taken for granted today, this was quite an achievement for any hybridiser at the time. 'Jane Myers' still pops up on the showbench and is recommended by leading breeders as a good parent plant.

Joel (Blue Self/Any Other Colour Self) is one of those colours which glows, catches the eye and causes dissension amongst its admirers, for it is more purple than blue and has been shown in both the classes for Blue Self and a Self of Any Other Colour. It grows strongly and sets off its striking blooms with well-silvered foliage. Like most of the blue colours amongst the Selfs, it may shade a bit but it is an attractive plant and deserves to be grown for its own sake.

John Wayne (Light Centre Alpine) was bred by Len Bailey, a grower normally associated with numerous Double seedlings which were highly successful from the 1970s into the current century, and was first put on display in 1979. It provoked much comment and admiration but initially proved to be not the easiest plant to cultivate. It has staged something of a comeback, but other equally bright varieties had made their debut in the intervening years and it is no longer quite such a sensation. It remains, however, a bright plant with

John Wayne

Joy

a good tube and eye and a solid magenta to plum base which runs through a broad central area of a bright magenta before petering out to a very pale shade right at the edge of the petals. This is a plant to place at the front of a group if you want to catch the attention of those passing by.

Joy (Light Centre Alpine) is a real veteran, having been presented to the world for the first time in 1931. It may not have all the attributes of some of the most recent Light Centres, but it is still a plant of character, derived chiefly from its striking crimson colour which shades less than most newer varieties. It appears on the showbenches and has a home in many a collection, having been used widely for hybridising and not providing too much by way of a challenge to the cultivator's skills.

Julia (Green Edge Show) was bred by Les Rollason from a 'Chloë' x 'Geldersome Green' cross. It has a variable track record. Some growers consider it a plant of some quality, while others dismiss it as a 'once every five years' plant. If you can persuade it to thrive for you, it has a golden tube, striking paste and black body. The green of its edge is a little lighter than some and it is this distinction that appeals to its

proponents. The scape may sometimes be a little too squat and the pedicels may extend further than they should but the truss will still catch your eye in the privacy of your own greenhouse, if not on the showbench.

Jupiter (Green Edge Show) is another Mozart symphony which ended up as a David Hadfield auricula. The raiser always considered this plant as one of high quality, but it is not an easy plant to bring to its best. It throws numerous watery shoots round the collar, leaving insufficient energy for the plant to build up a strong crown from which may emerge a stem strong enough to carry the quality blooms. The removal of these shoots leaves wounds that may permit the ingress of disease organisms, and yet this must be done if the grower wishes to see the plant in its full majesty. When grower and plant are working in harmony, a stout stem holds up a truss of half a dozen pips with a smooth-rimmed,

Jupiter

Kevin Keegan

golden tube, solid white paste, black ground with fine feathering and little flashing up the margins, and a bright green edge, all nearer to the 1-3-6 ratio seen all too infrequently in Green Edges. The only fault to which the pip is prone lies in the configuration of its petals. These are broader than on many other Greens and overlap nicely, but they can produce bull-nosed petals to mar the regularity of the truss.

Kentucky Blues (Double) merits its name. The blooms appear in shades of lilac blue. They do not carry as many petals as some of the button-eyed or curled-petal types, tending more towards the camellia form. They are borne in well-shaped trusses on strong plants carrying equally strong stems. The charming colour of 'Kentucky Blues' makes this plant stand out a little from the crowds. It is an attractive plant and a prize-winner too.

Kevin Keegan (Light Centre Alpine) was named for the England football star by a fellow denizen of the north-east of England, Derek Telford. It follows a line of similarly coloured Light Centre Seedlings from Mr. Telford, yet each one is subtly different in colour or form. It dates from 1983 and is a well-formed, worthy successor to 'Mark'. The centre is very light with a neat, round tube and a deep plummy maroon surrounding it. This shades out gradually into a bright mauve shade of pink at the petal edge. The whole plant is sturdy, though you may have to look out for long pedicels.

Kentucky Blues

Knights

Landy

Largo

Kiowa (Red Self Show) – *see* 'Cheyenne'

Knights (Red Self Show) is a striking shade of red. It was bred by Trevor Newton who has produced a number of good Self Show Auriculas. It has mealed foliage which serves as a good foil to the bright colouring of the pips. It is a known prizewinner, but may cause the cultivator some problems for it may sometimes rot off at the collar and leave the grower with a good cluster of small offsets. The other potential fault is a tendency for the paste to flash out up the edge of the petal, thus giving a starry look to its brilliant whiteness. It must be stressed that this does not occur on each pip and a well-shaped example is a joy to behold for this is a warming colour.

Landy (Gold Centre Alpine) is regarded by most Alpine enthusiasts as a 'good doer'. It has no particular vices and grows quite freely. It is a bright red with an intensely dark zone round the golden centre. Its well-formed pips have won it a good number of awards. The name comes from the American father-in-law of Mr. Telford's daughter, but Orlando, like his plant, is known to all as 'Landy'.

Langley Park (Light Centre Alpine) hovers on the edge of the top Light Centre Alpines. Its broad petals are a pink-mauve. The eye is quite small, emphasising the coloured outer area. While not outstanding as a single exhibit, it is widely used by exhibitors in multi-pot classes at national shows.

Largo (Gold Centre Alpine) is possibly the highest point in the development of the Hill Gold Centres by Allan Hawkes. It has won numerous awards over its lifetime since 1969 and will probably win more for those fortunate enough to acquire an offset, for these are in very short supply. It is one of those plants which seems intent on living in splendid isolation, for offsets are rare. It is also not always the easiest plant to cultivate. In good form, however, it is a joy to behold. The neat, round tube and shining golden eye stand in the centre of a dark, coppery brown ring which quickly becomes orange before it shades out equally quickly into a broad outer zone of the lightest orange. The brightness and circularity of the individual pips mark them out for special attention. Look for this one and admire it, and, should you be fortunate enough to be offered even the tiniest piece, be sure to make your gratitude very clear to the donor.

Lavenham (Any Other Colour Self) at first glance looks for all the world like the 'Chanel' trio of varieties but, when put next to these three, stands out immediately as a distinct colour. It came in fact from a different cross but still with the aim of producing a good Pink Self. It takes its name from the Suffolk village with houses of various colours including this one. It contains less mauve in its make-up than 'Chanel', 'Chiffon' and 'Taffeta' and is a more eye-catching colour. It also tends to shade less than the other three. It may prove a little more prone to dying off, but is well worth persevering with.

Lee Paul (Gold Centre Alpine) is a seedling from 'Sirius'. Its form for exhibition purposes is superior to that of its parent but its dark brown colouring lacks the flamboyance which one expects of the Gold Centres. Its dark brown overall cast may not be to everyone's taste, but, if it does please your eye, remember that on the showbench the judges have to consider form as one of the most important factors.

Limelight (Any Other Colour Self) is another of the great auriculas which we owe to Tim Coop. It is bred from, and closely resembles, 'Moonglow' with a very similar coloration but just a little paler in its serene creamy-green. Even the foliage is close to that of its renowned parent. Its attitude to life, however, is somewhat different, for whereas 'Moonglow' grows with gusto, 'Limelight' is slightly more reticent. Offsets are not produced so freely and the plant may either throw up a long carrot above the compost or even rot off at the collar. You may even discover a ring of a greenish shade round the paste instead of the unshaded cream which is demanded for show purposes. If you can discover the right *modus vivendi* with 'Limelight', you will be rewarded with a truly beautiful sight and one which I, for all the effort needed, would not be without.

Limelight

Lincoln Bullion

Lincoln Bullion (Double) is a bright yellow from Derek Salt. From long experience in the horticultural trade, Derek knows that it is all too easy to launch a new variety before it has settled down. There is an unfortunate history of newcomers which have all the characteristics of out-and-out champions in their first season and then lose their glory in the following years. He therefore keeps his new plants under wraps until he is sure that they will continue to prosper. Here is a good, lively yellow with smooth, rounded petals and a full, tightly closed centre to add to your collection.

Lincoln Chestnut (Double) is another new raising by Derek Salt. It has been shown with a full truss of neatly curled pips which fully live up to its name. The hint of white farina at the base of the petals enhances the richness of the outer zones. This is a handsome plant and has begun to collect awards on the showbench including the accolade of Best Plant in Show at the Northern Show of 2009.

Lovebird (Grey Edge Show) dates back to 1908. It has played a part in the breeding of fairly recent varieties but is not a plant to be recommended for its quality today. Though its edge is a good grey, the body colour is too narrow and the tube far too wide and crenated. It may appeal to some enthusiasts for its antiquity.

Margaret Martin (Grey Edge Show) is a plant which is decried by the purists but which stubbornly refuses to move out of the top flight. Its parentage is 'Lovebird' x 'Teem'. Peter Ward, a great connoisseur of Show Auriculas, deemed its form on its first appearance in 1973 to be of the very best. Since that time, few have persuaded it to abandon all of its foibles, yet many have shown it as a prizewinner. Peter described it neatly as 'an improved Lovebird'. Its tube is definitely weak. It is of the proper width, though it may become too wide on occasions, but its periphery can be spoilt by the crenations which run around its edge. The paste is good and white and the body a solid

Lincoln Chestnut

Margaret Martin

black, though it may become too narrow and allow the edge and the paste to touch, a fault in any edged variety. The grey of the edge is even and bright. The main advantage of 'Margaret Martin' is her appetite for life and her perennial ability to put up stout trusses of open blooms. This is one of the easiest plants to grow and any new grower should add this to his or her collection. Despite the variable form, 'Margaret Martin' has figured in prize-winning exhibits and, despite the protestations of some respected figures in the auricula world, looks likely to continue to do so.

Marigold (Double) is both famous and infamous in the world of the auricula, for its origin and its continued existence have both been less than usual. It came from the hands of the legendary grower, Dr. Robert Newton, some time around 1960. He raised it as the second generation from a cross between a double seedling given to him by his renowned sparring partner, Tom Meek (the redoubtable 'Teem'), and a perfectly standard Green Edge. The frilly, fully double, sterile creation of a strange mustard colour was dubbed 'Marigold', presumably due to its resemblance to the French variety of the said flower. It provoked either stunned amazement or profound disgust amongst all those who saw it at the time (and is still liable to do so today). It soon became known as both an oddity (under the sobriquet of 'the khaki horror') and as a rarity, for it rarely bore a single offset and by the 1980s was reduced to a single plant. Micro-propagation was just becoming known and 'Marigold' became one of the first auriculas to be subjected to the procedure. Fortunately, it was also one of the varieties which was amenable to the new science and stock became readily

available. Since that time 'Marigold' has remained readily available and a much better performer than in its earlier days. A word of caution is in order here, however: 'Marigold' has been one of the plants which have demonstrated that micro-propagation is not the perfect remedy that many hoped and claimed it might be when it first arrived on the scene. No less a stockist than Brenda Hyatt once brought to a northern show three plants of 'Marigold' newly flowering after their emergence from the laboratories. One was pale yellow, one was almost orange and one was the true mustard colour. Brenda warned all those to whom she showed the plants that this might well happen to other varieties. Reputable specialist nurseries will have the true plant if that is what you are seeking. Other suppliers may also have it, but it might be wise to see a pot in flower before you decide to make a purchase.

Mark (Light Centre Alpine) was the sensation amongst the Light Centres of the 1970s. It was bred by Derek Telford whose prolific supply of new introductions, mainly amongst the Alpines, was a hugely significant feature of the last quarter of the twentieth century. Its vigour and its consistent standard of bloom meant that a plant of quality soon became readily available and competition on the showbench became a matter of the grower's skill. It also meant that 'Mark' could be readily grown as a fine feature at the front of a garden border, needing only good drainage and appropriate division every couple of years. 'Mark' has a neat round tube with pleasing anthers and a nice, bright eye of a creamy white surrounding it. If an individual specimen becomes too vigorous, the eye can easily become too large and dominant. The dark crimson next to the eye forms a neat zone which eases its way out to a light, creamy pink at the edge. A truss of seven bright pips, held neatly on firm footstalks, is a beautiful sight. If grown too blowsily, the pips can become disproportionately large and lose their charm. The petal junctions will also cut into the eye.

Marigold

Mark

'Mark' has lost some of its initial quality as other similar varieties have become available, but, if you are just setting out into the world of auriculas, try this one.

Mary (Double) is one of the old originals, dating back to 1961, when it sprang from a packet of seed sent from Ralph Balcom in the USA to Mr. Gould in England. It possesses a modest creamy yellow shade which still stands well in contrast to the brighter colours. Although still seen every now and then on the showbenches, its penchant for exposing the tube at the centre of the blooms usually rules it out from the very highest awards. It is still capable of producing seed, however, and is kept by some who know how difficult it can be to persuade either pollen or seed from the most up to date and very full varieties. 'Mary' is available from good commercial suppliers.

Matthew Yates (Double) is one of the most widely available Double Auriculas. It was bred as long ago as 1980 by Len Bailey who grew many of his plants outside with minimal protection and who was one of the first enthusiasts to take up the breeding of well-formed Doubles. It is a plant of striking contrasts, for from its mealy foliage springs a strong scape which is topped by a full truss of cupped pips of the darkest burgundy maroon, so dark that the immediate impression is an array of black pips against the pale background of the leaves. In one's own garden the plant may be forgiven for the notches which may be seen on some petals and for the drooping blooms, for the pips are so heavy that the pedicels may not be strong enough to support them adequately. For exhibition purposes these are not in the plant's favour. In the hands of good cultivators who know how to inspire 'Matthew Yates' to overcome these potential faults, good show plants are possible and do gain the prize cards. If you are seeking a plant which will always provoke comment and do not intend to exhibit every pot, this is worthy of your consideration.

Mehta (Light Centre Alpine) derives its name from the conductor, Zubin Mehta, though it is often encountered under the misspelling of

Mehta

'Metha'. It is of reliable constitution and well regarded by leading showmen, having the ability to put up a head of good pips with others to come in reserve or to be culled for the best exhibition trusses. The tube and eye are neat and circular, while the coloured outer area sets out from a quite narrow band of plum-crimson and quickly shades out into a mid rosy pink, fading finally into a delicate rose pink. This is a sturdy and sound variety.

Metis (Double) is an introduction from Derek Tilt, the breeder of 'Prima' and a number of other leading Doubles. It throws a close truss of lilac-mauve pips, each with a cream base. The pips are round and the truss full. It is a frequent winner at shows and a sturdy grower. For exhibition purposes it may be necessary to remove any pips which start to encroach upon their neighbours. For general enjoyment, the amateur might just leave most of them to spread out their flowering spell.

Michael Wattam (White Edge Show) is named after the son of Paul Wattam, who crossed two very old varieties, 'The Miller' and 'True Briton'. The edge is very white, though the petals may come pointed. The body colour is a good black but too often carries flecks of meal. Tube and paste are quite good. There are not many plants of this variety in circulation though it may be worth hunting one down if you wish to breed White Edges.

Mikado (Dark Self Show) – *see* 'The Mikado'

Minley (Fancy), a Douglas seedling of the 1980s is one of a number of green-edged, cerise-bodied Fancies which can only be described as rough in form but catch the eye through their colouring alone. All tend to throw pointed petals and broad, usually

Metis

crenated tubes. The paste is solid and white. The plants attempt to throw numerous offsets round the collar which results in a weak central stem and a tendency to rot off at soil level. They are a source of different colours for the enthusiast looking for an outcross from the customary breeding lines, but, should you be tempted to go along this route, be aware that the sudden appearance of an outstanding new variety is highly improbable and several generations will be needed before a worthwhile product rewards your efforts. Nevertheless it has been done, so 'Minley', 'Astolat' or any other member of the clan might be worth a look.

Minstrel (White Edge Show) was bred by Les Wright of Essex from Douglas seed. It is truly white with a good tube and paste but the meal-dotted body usually precludes it from the florist's consideration.

Mipsie Miranda (Double) was bred by Hazel Wood as long ago as 1980 and is still acknowledged as one of the leading varieties today. It carries fewer petals than some of the current varieties but they have a pleasing, neat lay, often imbricated. The colour is a delicate cream. It is a tribute to a plant belonging to a very rapidly expanding section to have persisted for such a time and still to feature amongst the prize-winners today. The intriguing name was taken from a dog belonging to Hazel and Chris (himself a prominent breeder of Gold-Laced Polyanthus and Show Auriculas).

Miss Otis (Any Other Colour Self Show) – *see* 'Eaton Dawn'

Moon Fairy (Fancy) was bred by Cliff Timpson, a President of the Midlands Sections of the N.A.P.S. It is very close in appearance to 'Fairy Moon', which is not surprising given that the two are sister seedlings. 'Moon Fairy' has so far attained greater popularity and is grown by a greater number of florists. The basic form of the pips is that which is to be found in the Self Show types. It has a small, neat, round tube with a good round paste which may have a hint of fuzziness to its outer edge, though this is not always so. The colour beyond the paste begins as a cream shade but quickly becomes suffused with a pale violet which intensifies in its hue as it spreads out gently towards the periphery of the petals. The pips are often nicely round, though they do have

Moon Fairy

Mipsie Miranda

a tendency to cup and to carry notches. In the eye of the purists, such a flower should not be permitted in public. In the eyes of many who just admire this serene mixture of disciplined colour, it is a thing of beauty. 'Fairy Moon' is slightly darker in colour.

Moonglow (Any Other Colour Self Show) has become one of the most widely grown auriculas since it was bred by David Hadfield in 1975. It was described by Frank Jacques, the great judge of the day, as a 'gem of a flower'. The description and the name say everything. 'Moonglow' is a sturdy grower, producing pleasantly mealed foliage and putting up a good truss of well-formed pips with minimum effort on the part of the cultivator. The blooms are of a delicate greenish cream with a delicate texture that can thin quickly in bright sunshine. It may throw a ring of a darker shade next to the paste but a strong plant kept out of the heat will preserve its texture well. The tube is well formed and the paste broader than on many Selfs (a failing to which too many plants in this group are prone). It provides

Moonglow

the growers with a good supply of offsets each year so that a stock may be built up without much difficulty. This is indeed a 'must have' variety.

Moselle (Green Edge Show) is named (despite the French spelling of the name) after the German wine that comes in green bottles. It was bred by Bob Taylor, Secretary and long-time Editor of the Northern Section of the N.A.P.S. Its parentage is 'Orb' x 'Hew Dalrymple', two widely different varieties. 'Orb' is dark green and sombre with a heavy body, while 'Hew Dalrymple' is a lighter green with a very fine line of ground colour. The result with 'Moselle' (and also its sister plant 'Grüner Veltliner') is a nice halfway house between the two. Bob has always been able to grow this one vigorously, a feat emulated by a small number of others, while

Moselle

I have tried twice to please it and failed, the plants rotting off on both occasions. A third attempt is under way with a much softer compost in an attempt to encourage greater root growth. If you can persuade 'Moselle' to thrive, you will have a pleasing plant which merits the prizes it has won.

Neat and Tidy (Dark Self Show), with 'Nocturne', dates back to Dr. Robert Newton in 1955. For more than twenty years they ruled the roost amongst the Dark Selfs. 'Nocturne' was considered by some to be the same plant as 'Neat and Tidy', while others held it to be very similar but slightly weaker in growth. Certainly it was seen much less frequently at the shows. Both are perceptibly redder than either 'The Mikado' or 'Barbarella'. 'Neat and Tidy' still makes the occasional appearance at the shows but it lacks the brilliance of the darker varieties, though there is still something of the velvety texture to its petals. The foliage of both varieties is of an unusually matt green background with a feathery pattern of farina laid on top, a feature which 'Neat and Tidy' passed on to its children.

Nickity (Gold Centre Alpine) is the pet name applied to the son of the plant's raiser, Cliff Timpson, when he was young. It is a sturdy plant with brown to dark orange colouring, a neat centre and a round tube, a little broader than some but still inside the accepted proportions. Though not an ostentatious plant, it is very popular on the showbench and figures frequently amongst the award winners.

Nocturne (Dark Self Show) – *see* 'Neat and Tidy'

Oakes Blue (Blue Self Show) emerged slightly later than 'Blue Jean' from the breeding programme of Mr. Telford in Huddersfield. It is a vigorous grower with a good coating of meal on the leaves. It puts up a sturdy stem which supports a full truss of pips. The tube is of a pale shade expected in the Blues, though pollen is not often a feature of the anthers. It may be obtained early in the life of the pip but the prospective hybridiser needs to seek it in good time. The pips may shade, as they do in just about all Blues, but they are of a solid, dark colour which adds a certain refinement and almost austerity to the blooms. This is a plant that stands out when placed next to others in one's own frame or greenhouse and, when unshaded, enhances the colour of any Grey Edge which it stands near.

Orb (Green Edge Show) dates back to 1970 and was bred by Dr. Duncan Duthie in

Oakes Blue

Shropshire. Though not often seen nowadays on the showbench, it can still put up its dark green, rather sombre pips in spring. It is round enough in outline but tends to reflex. Its edge is of the darkest, while the ground is thick and black. The paste and tube are good but help to lighten the pips. It is not a dependable plant for exhibition but finds a place in many collections because it is so different.

Orlando (Grey Edge Show) is a sibling of 'Iago' with which it shares some weaknesses but also the ability to win awards. The tube is more crenated than in 'Iago' but provides a basis for the pip's 1-3-6 proportions. The body is less broad and does not carry as much erratic flashing. The quality of the paste is good but it may be cut by the petal edges on some pips. The petals are insufficiently regular (as is the case with 'Iago') for 'Orlando' to gain the highest accolades for circularity of pip but they are acceptable enough. Nevertheless, it can be persuaded to make a good plant by some growers and you may just be one of them.

Paphos (Double) was bred by Keith Leeming in 1997. It is a truly handsome plant, putting up a fine truss of six or more pips with beautifully round outlines and full, opulent flowers of a wine red with a sprinkling of farina to add a hint of mystery to their beauty. Both the colouring and the form of the pips are strongly reminiscent of the old roses. This is a frequent collector of awards at the shows and attracts comments wherever it appears.

Paris (Green Edge Show) is a Green Edge of Hadfield raising from about the time of 'Prague' and 'Haffner'. Though originally very promising, the raiser gave up this plant as others he considered better emerged from the breeding programme.

Pequod (Light Centre Alpine) is a controversial variety. It is the plant most often shown in classes for a Laced Alpine Auricula at shows staged by the Midlands and West Section of the N.A.P.S. Tradition dictates that the colour on the face of an Alpine Auricula should shade out gradually from the darker zone towards the eye. It was felt by Midlands growers that a more abrupt change in the colour was also acceptable, given that edged Show Auriculas and Laced Polyanthus are both long revered forms of primula. A small number of plants have been introduced which demonstrate this feature but only 'Pequod' manages to put in a regular appearance at the shows. It is usually a modest plant with none too large a truss. The pips have

Orlando

Paphos

a larger tube than usual, which reduces the flat area of the centre. The colour at the base is a rich purple plum which shades out quite abruptly to a narrow band of pale rose pink round the periphery. The petals are quite broad with a generous overlap.

Perdito (Green Edge Show) is a Hadfield plant still finding its way amongst the growers with a number of awards to its credit. It is a sturdy grower putting up a stout stem carrying rather short pedicels which may tend to crowd the pips a little. These, however, appear in a healthy truss of six or seven. The tube is round and of a fine gold. The paste is a little narrower than some might wish, though it still makes up a 1-2-4 proportioned bloom. The body is quite dark and feathers well into the broad light green of the edge. Each petal is nicely rounded and the outline of the whole pip is pleasantly circular too. Although usually shown as 'Perdito', the name is more likely to refer to Perdita, a central character in Shakespeare's *A Winter's Tale.*

Piers Telford (Gold Centre Alpine) owes its name to a member of the raiser's family. This is a plant with a real zest for life, growing vigorously and throwing up large trusses of sizeable pips. Herein lies one of its vices and virtues. If you let the plant get out of hand, it will throw a globular truss of pips which reflex and so lose their flatness. Grown as a garden plant, this may prove a bright addition to the edge of a border, looking very much like an orange-brown form of *Primula denticulata,* but for the showbench it is best to look for a fresh, young plant with flat blooms which just touch each other. The tube is a little wide but is still in good proportion to the rest of the pip. The eye is round and golden, while the colour is, as just mentioned, a pleasing mixture of brown and orange.

Pikey (Grey Edge Show) is a recent plant from Bob Taylor with a good scattering of meal overlying a quite dark edge tissue giving a

Piers Telford

dignified, classical look to a very promising variety. This plant is still the preserve of a few lucky recipients, but it is to be hoped that it becomes much more generally spread. The name comes from the youngest member of the *Dad's Army* squad in the British television series.

Prague (Green Edge Show) constitutes one of the highest points of David Hadfield's long career in breeding new auriculas. Up to the point of its introduction in the 1970s, Green Edged Auriculas had a reputation for being more than a little difficult to grow and for lacking vigour. The introduction of 'Prague' changed that, for here was a strapping plant which grew with gusto, provided plentiful offsets and was oblivious to its geographical location. Its tube is round in a good shade of yellow, the paste is of excellent quality and its ground is black with neat feathering into the bright green edge. The colour tends to run up the edges of the individual petals, while the rim of the petals is too pronounced in the eyes of some. The pips sometimes have a tendency to remain cupped, though on a good plant they will open flat. The strength of the growth is the main potential weakness of 'Prague' for, if allowed to grow too strongly or if over-fed, the

Prague

pips may come coarse, lose all their flatness and exaggerate any small weakness in its composition. Having said all that, if you are seeking a Green Edge without too many foibles and which will reward you with beautiful blooms, choose 'Prague' as one of your first acquisitions. It remains one of the best.

Prima (Double) is an aptly named plant from one of today's most prominent breeders, Derek Tilt. It rarely appears on the showbench without an award card before it and has gained the highest accolade of Best Plant in Show. It makes a squat, vigorous plant with a bold scape and strong pedicels which support strong trusses of neat pips which are usually seen just touching each other and forming a classical head. The colour is a striking, pale, greenish yellow which somehow catches the sun in spring. It does not offer as many offsets as one might wish and you may well have to wait in a queue to obtain one. Better still, prove to one of the growers that you can grow and show lesser varieties and then enquire as to availability. You may find that you are rated above those who are less proficient.

Prince Bishops (Blue Self Show) derives its name from the former rulers of Durham,

home of Trevor Newton who gave us this Blue Self. It possesses a dark, opulent version of the blue of the auricula and the mealy foliage which decorates most of the Blues. The plant initially threatened to carry all before it but has been less dominating of late. It is still a handsome thing in flower but it may decide to bloom early or to rot off at the collar. Despite these failings, offsets are produced in good quantity and there should always be a stock to hand, should a suicidal grip take hold of any particular pot. The richness of the pips will always induce any exasperated grower to persist with 'Prince Bishops'.

Prince John (Gold Centre Alpine) dates back to 1916 and can still make an attractive plant, though less so on the showbench at present after the spate of new introductions of high quality. It came from James Douglas but its parentage is a mystery. That may go some way to explaining its odd colour, for the plant only just slips on to the right side of the dividing line between Gold Centres and the amorphous group normally referred to by the cognoscenti as 'Custard Centres', a halfway house between Gold and Light. Its tube and centre are of reasonable size and shape but the coloured

Prince Bishops

Prince John

outer area, which has a dark enough base, becomes very pink for a Gold Centre as it shades out towards the rim. It has been used with some success as a pollen parent. Only a very good plant would be seen in competition, but, given its easy-going nature, it is not surprising to find it in many collections and readily available from commercial sources.

Prosperine (Green Edge Show) was one of the last plants bred by Ken Whorton, more usually associated with a whole string of the very best Doubles than with Green Edges. 'Prosperine' has a slightly different look from many other Greens. Its habit is altogether more slender and delicate. The straight stem stands up from narrower leaves than are to be seen on most Greens. The trusses too are that little bit smaller and more delicate. The pips have some crenation round the edge of the slim tube but this is not pronounced for the rim is noticeably round. The paste is bright white with a diameter which contributes to the pip's 1-3-6 proportions. The body is a good black and feathers out well into the willow green of the edge. Odd double-width petals may occur, as

they will on nearly all edged plants, but not in sufficient quantity to mar the quiet refinement of this excellent plant.

Ptarmigan (White Edge Show) is a relatively recent variety bred by Tim Coop and still not to be found in many collections. It carries a broad White Edge to its petals with a slightly narrow but solid black body. The paste is a good width and of excellent quality, while the tube is a lighter shade of yellow and nicely round. The broad edge means that the pips go a little beyond the classical 1-3-6 proportions but a good head of pips makes this an eye-catcher.

Quarry Lane (Light Centre Alpine) is a 1990s introduction which is acquiring a considerable following amongst leading proponents of the Alpine Auricula. It bears more than a passing resemblance to the much loved 'Sandra'. Its colour is a similar rich purple, shading out to a narrower ring of lilac round the edge of the petals. Both eye and tube are white and neatly formed. Its appearances on the showbench have shown it to be a good grower with a good truss of six or so pips.

Prosperine

Rag Doll (Fancy) too often lives up to its name, being a more ragged version of 'Fanfare'. It has a good, smooth, round tube and paste with a broad red body. The red flashes out too much, however, and also runs up the side of the petals. 'Rag Doll' is also more temperamental than 'Fanfare' with a more untidy habit of growth. Despite all these criticisms, if you come across an offset and you want to see a bright red with a white edge, all standing out against clean, well-mealed foliage, it is worth growing.

Rajah (Fancy) rarely appears in presentable form on the showbench but it is frequently encountered amongst the collections of many a grower. It originated from the House of Douglas alongside a number of other Green Edges with a red ground but is more persistent in its will to live than the rest. Its attraction lies in the huge contrast between its bright green edge and its fiery red (though broad) body colour when the pip first opens. Only rarely will the petals give up their desire to be either frilly or pointed and, while the paste is bright, the tube lacks refinement. It is therefore an even greater pity that the edge soon fades from its bright green to an unsightly straw shade on the pips first out, thus marring any uniformity in the truss. Very occasionally a plant may be seen which has been caught at the peak of its freshness. This will draw many a prospective grower, and even some who may not wish to concede the attractions of 'Rajah'. These odd occasions are much to be savoured. Seedlings from 'Rajah' may bear a similar red colouring to the parent but hybridists should be aware that some batches may also come predominantly black, while well-proportioned, circular form is a forlorn hope. If you wish to catch the combination of edge and body colour, you may then have to wait for the second or even third generation of seedlings before this recurs. Why then, you may ask, is 'Rajah' worth a mention, let alone a place in a collection? If you once see it at its most striking, you will understand.

Reynardyne (Double) made its debut only in 2007 but looks like becoming a regular at the national shows. As another product from Ed Picken, it should have a happy future, for his experience has helped him to present to the enthusiasts varieties which have both quality and staying power. Provided that nothing untoward occurs in the immediate future, this

Rag Doll

Rajah

Reynardyne

plant should gradually come into the hands of more than just the co-operative of Doubles breeders who, like those who breed plants in other sections of the auricula family, let out their new offerings to those who have helped them in the past. 'Reynardyne' is a tidy plant with strong growth and firm pedicels which carry their beautiful, very full blooms of orange brown over cream in stout heads. The lay of the petals again calls to mind the formation of many of the most shapely old roses.

Roberto (Green Edge Show) is an on-going reminder of its distinguished breeder, Dr. Robert Newton, who produced many of the Greens seen on the benches in the middle of the twentieth century. It has been viewed with suspicion by many growers, as its parents are believed to be 'John', another of Dr. Newton's Green Edges, and 'Teem', an outstanding Grey bred by his sparring partner in words, the Northern Section's editor, Tom Meek. Most crosses between two plants of differing edges will produce offspring that are themselves somewhere between the two but lacking either

the pure, serene green of one type or the quiet refinement of the other. For many years it was recommended that it should not be used in crosses, the theory being that its genes would inevitably lead to seedlings which were without value. More recently a number of first-rate plants have begun to appear with 'Roberto' as one of the parents. 'Roberto' is not an easy plant to acquire and just as problematical to grow. Offsets are usually very small and may linger for two or three years before they decide to grow away. The plant itself shows yellow blotches in the foliage which look like virus infection and the central cone to which the plant shrinks during the winter looks decidedly fragile. If you offer 'Roberto' conditions to its liking then it will put up a long scape in the spring which may bear from four to ten pips. Often the larger number means that the size is small and the form variable but a truss made up of fewer pips can be a thing of great beauty. The tube is

Roberto

smooth and a bright yellow and, with the pure white paste, helps to constitute the 1-2-4 proportions of many Greens. The body is a fine, solid black which feathers out finely into the bright green edge. The petals are smooth-edged and of a mid- to light green, their edges being quite regular. Young plants have a tendency to come with the line of meal round the periphery of the petals known as a 'China Edge'. This is usually deemed a fault, but the North East Show has a class for varieties of this kind. Grown well and strongly, this feature will disappear on mature plants when a most beautiful and distinguished truss faces the world. Such a plant was shown paired with the Grey 'Margaret Martin' to form an outstanding two-plant exhibit by Ken Whorton in 2005 which will long be remembered by those present that day.

Rodeo (Gold Centre Alpine) is another of C.F. Hill's 'o' series of Gold Centres. Its colouring is typical of the family, dark brown going out to orange. Its form has suffered as it has aged and it is not a plant for exhibition but it is worth considering by those interested in collecting the golden oldies (or in optimistically deploying their pollen).

Rowena (Light Centre Alpine) was one of the darlings of the florists in the 1970s and '80s. It is a neat, graceful plant with blooms to match, never becoming coarse or blowsy. The colour is very similar to that of 'Mark' (not surprising, since Rowena is one of that variety's parents) being a good crimson, soon shading out into a delicate light pink. The trusses can be counted upon to carry a generous number of pips and the plants have few vices. Newer varieties come and go but Rowena is always a reliable variety for personal enjoyment.

Royal Mail (Red Self Show) is well-named for its red would match any post-box. On its earliest appearances this was a plant which outshone all competition but it has now taken to producing a handsome specimen, filling a 3½in. (9cm) pot and then allowing its central cone to shrink to the point where it can no longer throw a respectable truss of bloom. As with most auriculas, this is not always so and when it decides to adhere to its earlier, more sober pattern of growth, it throws up a strong scape carrying a good head of bright red pips with a golden tube and fine white paste. The light green foliage is practically meal-free. Its freedom of offsetting permits the grower to keep a constant stock on the go, always in the hope that it might revert to its prime form.

Rowena

Royal Mail

Samantha

Sandra

The prospective breeder is fortunate in that 'Royal Mail' is free with its pollen which takes well. He or she should, however, be wary of seedlings from such crosses growing vigorously at first and then persistently splitting their crowns at soil level.

Samantha (Double) was bred by Ben and Hazel Nottingham and has become a firm favourite of the top ranks of Doubles growers. It is a very full flower of a delicate flesh-pink over a pale buff base, delightful to see and more difficult to define. The leaves on this variety are matt and carry a small amount of farina, unlike many others of recent introduction.

Sandra (Light Centre Alpine) owes its origins to a southern breeder, Mr. Warriner, who sent seed to Hal Cohen, for many years the Secretary of the Midlands Section of the N.A.P.S. Hal was a grower of the highest quality but produced few plants of his own breeding. From this donated seed, however, emerged in 1972 one of the great Alpine Auriculas. For a number of years the plant carried all before it and was not easy to

come by. Today it is readily available and, despite numerous new introductions since the 1970s, can still carry off the top awards. The tube is neat and round with a small, bright eye. The body starts off as a solid area of dark lilac-mauve which occupies a striking, broad zone across each petal before easing out into a lighter mauve. The seven or eight petals which make up the pip are very regular in size and build up a nice, circular bloom. Generous numbers of pips compose sturdy trusses on good length stems. Its very regularity of formation makes it an ideal proposition for those enthusiasts who dress their flowers. Dressing is a procedure admired by some and decried by others. It involves ensuring that each petal of a pip overlies but one side of its neighbour with each petal overlying the same edge as the next, so, for example, the left-hand edge of each petal is slightly covered by the right-hand edge of the one next to it. This forms a pinwheel pattern round the pip. The result, if successful (and that requires considerable dexterity), constitutes the height of symmetry in the eyes of some and horrible artificiality to others. 'Sandra' grows strongly, despite a tendency for some plants to rot off, and provides a good supply of offsets round the collar of the plant. These may need to be controlled to produce a strong central crown. The surgery involved may be one of the causes of rotting off. If you wish to grow Light Centres, 'Sandra' is one of the varieties you must try.

Sandwood Bay (Gold Centre Alpine) appeared, alongside its sibling, 'Applecross', in 1971. Both are the same striking colour of almost black shading out to a bright crimson red. The bright yellow centre stands out in contrast at the centre of the pips. Both took up the mantle of 'Blossom' as the great red Gold Centres for a time in the 1970s and '80s, though both began to show quirks after that. Neither is now as vigorous as when they were at their prime and they no longer appear frequently at the shows, but both make very attractive pots of bloom. 'Sandwood Bay' was always the better of the pair but either would provide this colour in any situation.

Sappho (Green Edge Show) is one of the most recent Hadfield line of Greens and continues to enjoy the vigour of a youngster. Because it was introduced quite recently, it may not be easy to come by an offset but if it continues to thrive, as it is at the moment, it should become more widespread in a short time. Its form is very good. It has a fine, bright yellow tube with just a hint of crenation but nicely cupped below the anthers. The paste is smooth and solid and surrounded by a regular, black ground. The petals are a pleasing mid-green and noticeably regular in their formation. A truss of five to seven pips is an impressive picture. Auriculas have a nasty habit of deteriorating in health for no apparent reason. Let us hope that such a fate does not befall 'Sappho', for it is a beautiful auricula.

Sarah Gisby (Double) is a dark lilac purple with much of the colour of a gallica rose but a

Sandwood Bay

slight difference in its form. Gone is the button or quartered eye of the rose and in these pips one finds scrolls of petals curving sinuously around the crown at the centre or a more formal, camellia-formed configuration. The fresh green of the leaves and the vigorous habit of the plant enhance the appearance of a well-grown specimen. Exhibitors may have to keep an eye on the uniformity of colour across the truss but this applies to many Doubles. 'Sarah Gisby' is a fine plant and appeals to both exhibitors and to those who take their florist's art less competitively.

Sarah Gisby

Scipio (Green Edge Show) is a rarely seen Green Edge, again from David Hadfield. In best form it has a round, golden tube, solid paste (though a little fuzzy on its extremity) and a reasonable body and edge. It is not always inclined to throw pips of this sort but is worth persisting with, if you have the knack.

Scorcher (Red Self Show) lives up to its name. It is one of Tim Coop's greatest achievements. The fiery red of its blooms shines out amongst other plants. Red Selfs in the past tended to possess either good form and moderate colour or bright colour and weaker form. 'Scorcher' has both form and colour backed up with a robust habit. The tube is a light, bright gold, the paste is solid, very white and of admirable width. The petals are nicely rounded, of good texture and without shading or veins. A fine truss of five or six pips stands out well against the light green of the leaves, decorated as they are by a fine dusting of farina. The whole plant grows sturdily and offsets freely. This is another 'must-have' variety.

Serenity (Green Edge Show) is an old variety which is not up to show standards nowadays. The green edge and the body tend to be spattered with specks of farina.

Scorcher

Sharon Louise

Sergeant Wilson (Grey Edge Show) – *see* **Corporal Jones** and **Sergeant Wilson**

Sharmans Cross (White Edge Show) bears more than a passing resemblance to 'Brookfield', not surprising when one remembers that they are from the same stable. It carries a slightly lighter edge than 'Brookfield' but its overall quality is lower. It can also be more reticent to thrive. Its crenated tube often carries through into it seedlings bred from it. In view of the scarcity of White Edges, it may be worth a pot or two in your collection, but it is not to be relied on.

Sharon Louise (Yellow Self Show) created quite a stir when she arrived on the auricula scene. There were already several good Yellow Selfs but when Ken Bowser introduced 'Sharon Louise', a new and very vigorous bright yellow, it not only matched the competition, it often beat them at the shows. It grows with enthusiasm and throws a good quantity of offsets. It has a fine, round, golden tube which is neatly filled with anthers, a solid paste and thick yellow petals without shading or veining. The truss is held high on an unusually long but still robust scape. The truss can stand out head and shoulders above most other Show Auriculas. This can make it a difficult plant to fit into a row of pots for exhibition in a multi-pot class but it is a frequent winner in the Single Yellow classes. If you want to try just one of this type, this is a good plant to begin with.

Sherbet Lemon (Yellow Self Show) is yet another of the 'April Moon' group but much paler in shade and more delicate in its constitution. It stands on the borderline between the Yellow and the Any Other Colour groups, falling just on the right side. It has a hauntingly pale pip of good form and stands out in the company of the other brighter shades. If you can get hold of a plant and persuade it to thrive, treasure it.

Sirius (Gold Centre Alpine) was going to provoke controversy from the moment it first saw daylight. It came from one of the truly great north of England characters, Frank Jacques, in 1979. Frank could not say what its parentage was. He was uncustomarily diffident about placing it on the showbench, being unwilling to commit 'Sirius' to the Gold Centres, though the consensus of fellow growers in the hall was that its centre undoubtedly placed it in that category. The tube is slightly on the large side and may not be completely closed off by the anthers, while

Sirius

the eye may also be a little vague in its outline. The colouring varies slightly as the pips age, but it never ceases to be an admirably dark maroon red nearest to the eye. The darker area quickly shades out through a lighter hue to finish as a peach shade at the rim. The difficult aspect of the colour to catch in words is the hint of blue throughout it all. Gold Centres have no blues and yet it is just perceptible here. Immediately it was released it was in huge demand by other growers because it was so different and by the leading breeders who swiftly came up with other brown shades derived from it. The only problem became that the progeny tended to become increasingly gloomy. Even now a small number of new introductions lead one to suspect that 'Sirius' may be lurking a generation or so back in their parentage. It continues to be a robust grower and is easily obtainable from growers and commercial sources the length and breadth of the U.K. It can even hold its own in the garden border. If you are looking for an easy plant with more than a hint of character, try 'Sirius'.

Snowy Owl (White Edge Show) is reminiscent of the older White Edges which came down from the mid-1900s but carries larger pips than those varieties. The meal on the edges of those older types such as 'White Wings' and 'James Arnot' was very dense and heavy in comparison with more recent introductions. It could even tend towards being granular and coarse with a hint of cream to take away some of the brilliance. 'Snowy Owl' is whiter than that but still carries more meal on the pips than one would often wish, for it may besprinkle the body too, a serious failing in the eye of the florist when it occurs. The tube is a reasonable, if slightly dark, yellow and may be crenated. Despite these failings, good cultivators still come up with perfectly acceptable plants. And it may just be the jaundiced eye of those of us who cannot succeed with it that produces this opinion, for others would say that this is a genuinely good plant.

Sonny Boy (Gold Centre Alpine, also met with as 'Sunny Boy') is a brightly coloured Gold Centre with a dark scarlet-black base shading through red to a gentle orange. It is highly regarded by those who can induce it to flower to its best and not so popular with others for whom the outline of the centre is a little ragged. It is an attractive plant which can add colour to any group of auriculas.

Sophie (Light Centre Alpine) is an introduction amongst the ranks of the crimson to carmine types since 2004. It stands out for its depth of colour which adds a certain feeling of weight or gravity to a group of flowers. The well-formed centre is not always as light as the paler shades but it is still well within the Light Centre boundaries. The darkest zone around the eye is quite broad and fades out moderately towards the rim of the pip. The petals are smooth edged and build up into a good, round outline. The plant seems to grow with adequate vigour and its appearances amongst award-winning groups of Alpines make this a desirable plant.

Space Age – *see* 'Star Wars'

Spartan (Light Centre Alpine) shown by George Mander, won the Premier Award at the

Spartan

Knowle Show of the Midlands Section of the National Auricula Society in 2006. It is a vigorous plant of the plum-coloured persuasion but with blooms slightly different from others like it. The tube is just a little broader than many, as is the centre, but both are within the normally accepted criteria. The deep maroon adjacent the eye shades out nicely to the edge but never fades into the palest hue of its basic pigmentation. The whole pip retains a glowing darkness which distinguishes it from many others. This darker colouring does not become oppressive, however; it just sets this variety apart with a character of its own. This is definitely a plant to watch.

Spring Meadows (Fancy) and a near relative, 'Sweet Pastures', were seedlings of a Midlands enthusiast, Jack Ballard, in the 1950s. Both are Fancies with a yellow ground. 'Sweet Pastures' carries a grey edge to its pips, while 'Spring Meadows' is a Green. Neither can claim the best of form, though 'Spring Meadows' has a neater tube which may even be quite smooth and round on a strong plant. The body on both is too broad for them to be considered alongside the traditional 1-2-4 or 1-3-6 of the true Green Edges, but it this very failing which attracts many,

Sonny Boy

Spring Meadows

for 'Spring Meadows' has a medium to dark but shimmering green edge, while the ground is of a waxy yellow. The resounding contrast between the two ensures that the plant is often seen at the shows. It is an easy grower and, once acquired, provides a regular supply of offsets.

St. Boswells (Grey Edge Show) was never a plentiful plant, even in the 1970s when it was newly introduced. It is another child of 'Teem' and, like just about every other one, has inherited a slightly dubious tube from its parent with a mildly crenated outline. Its main fault is, however, a lack of general vigour and an indisposition towards production of offsets. Only in the hands of the most able growers has it been induced to show its true capabilities. When it does, apart from the tube, it has a good, white paste, a striking black body and a pale grey edge. The petals may be of slightly uneven sizes but the roundness of the pips sets up an attractive truss of bloom. The foliage may be of a lighter grey than many other varieties. This is definitely not a plant for the beginner or for those without much patience.

Star Wars (Fancy) was an early debutant in the long line of Fancies bred by Tim Coop. He had begun from practically nothing by way of genetic material but, by crossing between what he had and standard edged auricula lines, he gradually began to come up with plants showing the mealy edges of the Greys and Whites combined with the non-black bodies of the Fancies. 'Star Wars' has a grey edge and a violet body. It has many faults from the perspective of the exhibition varieties. The tube is sometimes large and crenated, the body is broad and flashes out too much and the petals are often far from round; but at the time of its first appearance almost nothing of this persuasion had been seen for nearly a hundred years. If you are new to auriculas and would like to grow something which will certainly be admired by all who catch sight of it, try 'Star Wars' for it is a general 'good doer' with few vices. Its sibling, 'Space Age', is similar but with an over-large tube and does not thrive to the same extent.

Stella North (Light Centre Alpine) is one of a pair of recent introductions by Dave Skinner. Both have become rapid favourites of the Alpine fraternity and both are popular exhibition varieties. The form and colour have been praised by all. The habit seems to be

Stella North

sound and offsets are beginning to circulate. A full head of pips may be seven or more and forms an impressive sight with a round tube set off by a slightly raised rim. The eye is good and pale but has been shown slightly corrugated. The colour is a very dark shade of lilac shading out quickly to a broad band of a light lilac pink. This is a really bonny plant.

Stella South (Light Centre Alpine) is another newcomer and of a similar colouring to 'Stella North'. Even the form is very similar. One difference may lie in the centre which is neat and very flat, though on occasions it may be seen to show just a trace of angularity. Both this and 'Stella North' derive their names from power stations. Both are considerably more attractive.

Stripey (Double) is not often encountered on the showbenches but, being from Derek Salt who has a habit of coming up with new twists to the usual breeding lines, one can be sure of something just that little bit different. The pips are much less full than the exhibition types and there may even be a hole at the centre, but the pips live up to their name. Over a cream base lie radial stripes of shades of purple with a good scattering of farina to add even more character to the blooms. While 'Stripey' may not be a prizewinner, it will always provoke comment and has been used to produce other striped doubles.

Sumo (Gold Centre Alpine) is a recent addition to the ranks of the Gold Centres and is popular with a number of leading exhibitors, though it has yet to find itself among the major award winners. It is a good brown/orange though its centre may sometimes lack a precise edge and it has been known to reflex.

Super Para (Dark Self Show) was amongst a whole batch of Dark Selfs which came from Derek Telford, more usually known for the huge string of Alpine Auriculas which came from his breeding programme. It is very similar to 'Neat and Tidy' of which it is a seedling.

Sumo

Never one to be too solemn on the topic of naming his new varieties, Derek also bestowed on another Dark Self the wonderful title of 'Gizabroon'. Being from the north-east of England, it is the manner in which he was accustomed to ask for a bottle of ale. This is again very similar to both 'Super Para' and 'Neat and Tidy', a good, sturdy plant and freely available.

Susannah (Double) is one of the oldest Doubles in existence. It came from Allan

Super Para

Sword

Hawkes in the early 1960s and is still in many collections. It needs a little care in cultivation, tending to offset rather more than is desirable, but if you can shape it into a single crown it will reward your care with a nice truss of fresh lilac-pink pips of quite good form, though more notched than plants of more recent breeding. Although the colour ages to a bluer shade, on its freshest day it is a delicate and fetching sight.

Sweet Pastures (Fancy) – *see* 'Spring Meadows'

Sword (Double) is never seen amongst the plants set up for competition at the national shows and yet it is in many collections and offered by most commercial suppliers. The reason for its odd situation is the fact that it is a Double Green Edged Show Auricula. It was bred by Derek Salt, one of the old hands of the auricula world, and appeared as an incidental by-product of a breeding line involving standard Green Edges, including the exhibitors' favourite, 'Prague'. It cannot be described as a handsome plant. The thin paste may just be

seen as each layer of petals emerges from where the tube would normally be found and the body colour is much broader than it would be in a normal Green Edge. The edge is thin but as green as could be asked for. Each of its many petals is pointed. Despite all this, 'Sword' is currently unique and grown by many florists just because of its cussedness and its easy-going nature. It is a strong plant, giving its offsets easily and in good quantity. It does not succumb to anything other than scandalous treatment and blooms every season, even on small plants.

Taffeta – *see* **Chanel, Chiffon and Taffeta**

Tamino (Green Edge Show) is the young prince in *The Magic Flute* and continues the Mozart theme which has flowed through the Green Edges. It is one of David Hadfield's last introductions and is shaping up to be one of the best. In just a few years it has become a favourite of growers for its outstanding blooms. For some reason, one or two of the

Tamino

best known names in the ranks of exhibitors had difficulty at first with this plant. The common complaint was that it refused to grow vigorously or just rotted off. Given a really open compost and never being allowed to dry out (not always the easiest regime to follow), it has since shown a wonderful constitution and a willingness to throw a good number of offsets, thus making it available to a wider circle of growers than some of the older Greens. The pip shows a roundish golden tube with the anthers set in a shallow cup; the paste is a solid white disc and is surrounded by a dark body of a good width. The petals are a bright green and regular in shape, adding an air of neatness to the truss. Five or more pips are common on a well-grown specimen in a truss which stands up firmly from the leaves at the base. This is a plant of the highest quality and is one of the Greens which you must try to cultivate.

Teem (Grey Edge Show) is one of those fabled varieties in auricula lore along with names such as 'Chloë' and 'The Mikado'. Its name is the nom de plume of Tom Meek, for many years the Editor of the Northern Section Yearbook and a renowned grower. Its parentage is unknown, since it probably resulted from a packet of Haysom seed. For twenty years after its introduction it dominated the Grey-Edged group then, after a period of decline, it began to re-emerge in the hands of skilled growers such as Bob Taylor and Richard Westwood. It is not an easy plant to cultivate but it brings its rewards for those growers who succeed. Its tube is crenated but shows a good, bright yellow. The paste and body are exemplary with an eye-catching contrast of white and black. The edge is an enigma; it may come a light, very bright grey or, if the farina is even more densely packed, as white. The result is that 'Teem' has gained top prizes in both classes. Some voices have been raised to complain that, if a plant is adjudged to belong to one group, it cannot migrate to another.

Teem

Fortunately, the judges have taken a far more pragmatic stance, awarding the prizes to a plant and not to a name. 'Teem' is not an easy variety to please. It demands perfect drainage and adequate moisture. It sends up a tall central stem which may obstinately refuse to produce roots and may look ungainly. It is also none too free with its offsets. Earlier in its life it was looked upon as the supreme pollinator, but today one finds few new Greys with 'Teem' as a pollen parent. Those which have arisen from it (such as 'Margaret Martin') tend to carry the same crenated tube. It is, however, a superb plant on its day and is worth a go, if you have the patience and – better still – the ability.

The Bride (White Edge Show) was introduced in 1959 by Fred Buckley who gave us the Green Edge, 'Chloë'. It is an odd plant, opting either to thrive or to seek another world for its happiness. It comes and goes as a show variety but, when in robust health and good form, still has the beating of most White Edges. If you should come by a plant which refuses to

The Bride

to the opinions of earlier growers, it will also set seed; this is not abundant but it does throw White Edges. Try this plant and see for yourself.

The Lady of the Vale (Gold Centre Alpine) was bred by Cliff Timpson, President of the Midlands and West Section of the N.A.P.S., from an 'Andrea Julie' x 'Largo' cross and takes its name from one of the steeples of Lichfield Cathedral. It was first shown in 1993 and has appeared frequently at the shows since then. Its desire to blossom is remarkable, for it has been seen on display with more than a dozen pips. In this form you are more than likely to see some angular centres and cupped pips, so a little thinning out may be needed for exhibition, but in your own frame or greenhouse (or even in your open garden) you might just wish to let this plant do its own thing. It carries splendidly bright flowers of dark, brownish red shading out quickly through red and orange to a pleasing apricot. It is typical of the raiser's seedlings to show a hint of being just that bit different from the majority.

prosper, try a very soft compost with a high proportion of soilless compost and an equally high proportion of a material such as Perlite to assist the drainage. It was my custom some years ago to grow young plants in a soilless compost without any further additions until they looked mature and strong. They were then potted on into a John Innes plus grit mix. This usually did the trick and they flowered well. The main problem was that thereafter they would sulk or pine away. A more recent experiment with a soft compost, but this time containing John Innes, is still under way and no firm conclusions can be drawn, but optimism persists. If you can induce the old lady to put up three or more full-sized pips, they will draw the eye from a distance. The tube is a darkish yellow, and usually reasonably smooth, and the paste is a brilliant white of a good texture and width. Between this and the genuinely white edge lies a broader than usual band of tar black which causes many an innocent passer-by to pause and admire the stark and beautiful contrast. The ground feathers out well into the white edge but may also wander a little too far up the edge of individual petals. Despite this potential foible, 'The Bride' remains one of the best, if you can persuade it to thrive. Contrary

The Mekon

The Mekon (Green Edge Show) is a 2005 variety from Brian Coop. After the earlier success of 'Benny Green', an impressive plant, Brian came up with a variety which, though still very new, shows all the signs of being even better, reminding some of the older growers of 'Chloë' in its early days, though with a lighter edge than that plant. The bright yellow, cupped tube is round and well-filled with anthers. The paste is a circle of fine, solid white, the ground is a good, well-feathered black and the edge round and composed of relatively broad petals. The foliage has a curl which may still be seen on the best plants of the old Buckley variety. If 'The Mekon' preserves its vigour and form, this is another 'must have' plant.

The Mikado (Dark Self Show) is one of the oldest auriculas in existence, dating back to 1906, and yet it is still capable of being grown to the highest standards. It is a plant which has thrived and shrivelled several times in the course of its long life. Each time it threatened to sink into oblivion a number of growers came up with a plant in which the will to live was re-affirmed. Having seen such a plant being grown under an apple tree by David Cornforth, a Lancashire horticulturalist, I can only wonder at what it was that each time induced 'The Mikado' to revive. Its leaves carry

Toffee Crisp

The Mikado

yellow marks which one suspects might be a manifestation of some physiological abnormality and yet it grows away happily. When it carries blooms of the proper size, they stand in wonderful contrast to the meal-free foliage. The pips are like those of 'Barbarella', of a very dark shade of red, approaching black, with a good, yellow tube and a shining white paste.

Toffee Crisp (Gold Centre Alpine) echoes the name of a popular item from the confectionery counter whose wrapper is printed in the same colours. The brightness of the colour makes this another one of those plants which seems to shine out amongst those around it. The tube is good and the golden centre a little smaller than is often the rule. The dark red at the base of the petals quickly yields to a narrow band of mid-red which then flows out to a broader area of light orange and it is this outer colouring that strikes the viewer from a distance. 'Toffee Crisp' is new but is finding its way quickly into many collections and crops up regularly amongst prize-winners at national shows. It promises a great future. The naming of this plant again reflects

Trouble

Upton Belle

something of the magnanimity of the National Society, for it was raised by Ken Bowser, passed on to John Cattle who gave a plant to Terry Atkinson who then named it after the wrapper of the confectionery bar.

Trouble (Double) is aptly named. It was originally one of a pair of seedlings, the other being 'Strife' which is no longer with us. The plant grows readily enough and sends up beautifully formed pips with an odd mixture of colours which does not appeal to all tastes. From a distance it may appear a pale shade of brown but a closer inspection will reveal yellow, pink and even some green in there too.

Upton Belle (Yellow Self Show) stands out amongst many Yellow Selfs with its thick petal texture. It has an unfortunate tendency to throw pips of a coarser form than one might wish with some twisted or notched petals. On those occasions when it behaves more decorously, its solid colour and shining paste make it a real winner. The foliage carries a reasonable layer of meal but it does not display the brightness of some other Yellows.

Vera (Gold Centre Alpine) is a new raising from Ken Bowser and looks to have a promising future. It grows easily and throws up well-formed trusses of seven- or eight-petalled pips of a blood red fading to bright orange or peach. The form and proportions of the rest of the pip are of the best and the anthers carry plentiful, bright pollen. It is just beginning to become widely available and should be seized upon, should you come across an offset. A brief scan through the results of any auricula show will reveal that it is a very successful exhibition

Vera

Victoria de Wemyss

plant. It is too early to say whether 'Vera' is tough enough for the open garden, but for an attractive addition to any collection this is a must.

Victoria de Wemyss (Light Centre Alpine) came from seed given to Jack Wemyss-Cooke by Derek Telford. It is one of those delightful pale mauve-blues which seem to radiate a gentle suffusion from the almost translucent zone at the edge of the petals. Once one of the best showbench varieties, it

Walhampton

has taken to a certain waviness round the periphery which has brought it down in the estimation of the exhibitors. Nevertheless, good specimens are still seen and it remains a beautiful sight amongst those plants of brighter colours.

Walhampton (White Edge Show) was bred in the New Forest by Cyril Haysom who named a number of his plants after places in the area. Originally highly thought of and being staged on the showbench into the 1980s, it is no longer considered a reliable variety for exhibition but will provide something different for the grower who is just looking for his or her own pleasure. It has an ungainly habit of throwing up a long carrot above the level of the compost. Its main fault for exhibition purposes is that the body is very narrow and, at times, missing so that the edge meets the paste. Both edge and paste are very white, however, and it was the quality of these that attracted the eye of Peter Ward in the 1970s when he used this variety, crossed with 'Teem', to produce such well-known plants as 'Warwick', 'Gavin Ward', 'Brookfield', 'Sharmans Cross' and 'Clare'.

Walton (Light Centre Alpine) is a fairly old variety, coming from Gordon Douglas in the 1950s. It is not a good variety for exhibition, being prone to a number of faults such as notched petals and angular or even colour-marked centres. It also lacks sufficient robustness for the grower to set it out in the garden border. What keeps it going is its colour which is a bright shade of blue, the nearest to a true light blue that any auricula is likely to attain and rare until the advent of 'Avril Hunter', 'Dilly Dilly' and 'Blue Yodeler'. When illuminated by warm spring sunshine, 'Walton' stands out amongst its companions for sheer brightness of hue.

Warwick (Grey/White Edge Show) is not an easy plant to grow, but those growers who do possess the endeavour and insight (or perhaps

Warwick

the magic touch) are rewarded with a supremely beautiful auricula. Bred by Peter Ward from a series of crosses involving 'Teem' and 'Walhampton', it has a sprinkling of the finest farina on its edge which shines towards the eye of the spectator. As with so much in life, this has two aspects: one is to render the plant serenely attractive, the other is to tip it over the border into the White Edged group. Indeed, 'Warwick' has been known to stand side by side on the showbench in the two separate classes with prize cards awarded to both. The reason for this is that the auricula judge adjudicates on the plants before him or her and not on the name under which they are shown (though in cases of false identification the judge may either write a note on the exhibitor's card or have a quiet word off the record later). The petals on a well-grown plant of 'Warwick' are very regular in their shape with fewer of the double or bull-nosed petals which all Edged Auriculas produce. Its body colour is a solid shade of black and lies in a neat ring round the gleaming paste. The tube is the weakest feature of the variety, for, despite being a bright gold, it is crenated round its rim, a feature left over from 'Teem', and slightly disturbs the simple circularity of the remainder of the pip. Another characteristic inherited from 'Teem' is the tendency to produce a long carrot which refuses to throw roots. This often leaves the grower with an ungainly palm-tree of a plant or he/she is compelled to attempt to bury the offending length of stem, an act which may sometimes encourage the production of new roots but may also lead to the onset of rot. 'Warwick' does produce offsets but not in any great quantity, so, should you acquire a plant, lavish your attention upon it and cherish every tiny offset you take from it.

Whistlejacket (Any Other Colour Self Show) is the best-known of a small group of experimental Brown Selfs produced by Brian Coop, a man to whom the auricula world owes a huge debt for his efforts (alongside his father, Tim) to widen the scope of the plants traditionally available. Brown remains a colour for much work and much disappointment in Brian's view. Of the plants he has produced in this range, 'Whistlejacket' is the only one to have made the grade so far. It is not the easiest grower, producing a couple of elongated main stems instead of the desired single crown. It

Whistlejacket

often refuses to root from these and then throws a truss of generally no more than three pips, thus making it difficult to put on the showbench, but, in one's own greenhouse or frame it is possible to forget the stringent pre-conditions of the exhibition hall and to enjoy the velvety mid-brown of the sumptuous blooms. The tube is passable, the paste may be slightly cut by the petal edges, but the combination of golden tube, white paste and that incomparable colour makes this a plant to acquire and savour.

White Satin (White Edge Show) is still a rarity but seems to be growing strongly enough to be in the hands of many growers. It comes from Alan Chadwick, a breeder of primulas and auriculas of all types. One promising characteristic is its ability to throw a decent number of offsets without the sort of proliferation which weakens the plant and can lead to the deterioration of both the central stem and any blooms which try to spring from it. Its first appearances brought widespread commendation for it was both sturdy, genuinely white and well formed with a good truss on a strong scape. The foliage is well mealed. It has not appeared too frequently since its debut but plants which have been seen away from the exhibition halls have borne out the initial quality. While it is still a little premature to pass a final judgement on 'White Satin', many are optimistic about its future.

White Wings (White Edge Show) is an older White Edge, coming from the House of Douglas in the 1930s. It is not a strong grower and rarely puts up a decent truss of bloom. The farina of both the edge and the paste can have a dull, creamy colour and the body may carry speckles of meal. It does represent, however, an earlier type of White Edge.

William Gunn (Double) comes from the breeding programme of Randall Dee. It is

William Gunn

another of the newer brown shades which have made such an impression on both florists and casual onlookers. It is now beginning to make its way into a wider circle of growers and examples shown by the experienced hands are fine plants. The habit of growth appears to be somewhat squat but the closely clustered truss is a beautiful sight with its rich brown shading out to an orange brown at the periphery, the whole showing a tantalising hint of farina on the reverse of the petals. Each pip is strongly reminiscent of some of David Austin's New English Roses.

Wincha (Dark Self Show) is something of an enigma. It is a good Dark Self but whenever I have grown it the pips have been marred by spikes of paste running out from the centre and up the edge of the petals (it looks for all the world like one of those stars which decorate many a Christmas card) and yet other growers have the ability to produce plants free of this defect. I have to admit to my failing here. If you see a well-grown plant, ask the grower for an offset.

STRIPES

Angel Eyes is a reliable plant which has few quirks and rewards anything like reasonable cultivation with attractive blooms and a reasonable supply of offsets. It merits that understated recognition given by many florists of being 'a good doer'. The tube is pale but carries a raised rim to lend a hint of finish and character. The paste is dense, white and round, though it may show a few radial lines. The colour is a solid mid-lilac with generous, mealy stripes overlying the pale tissue. Newer varieties have emerged from the breeding line since 'Angel Eyes' was first presented to the world but this one is a good plant to begin with.

Bittersweet is not likely to be readily available in the immediate future but stocks will no doubt become available as Mr. Parsons' generosity is known to all enthusiasts. It is a rare achievement for any auricula to throw a truss of eleven pips, let alone eleven which are of quality, and yet this is how the breeder staged 'Bittersweet' at the Knowle Show of the Midlands and West Section of the N.A.P.S. in

Bittersweet

2006 when it was judged to be the Best Stripe in Show. The foliage is nicely mealed but does not exhibit the whiteness of some others. The colour is reflected, however, in the blooms. The body is a pleasing pale purple which runs in numerous stripes out through the pip. The farinaceous strips form broader stripes of green grey which perfectly match their coloured counterparts. The pips also have the advantage of being quite smoothly edged without the nibbled effect of some other varieties. Tube and paste are as circular as one might come across in any Edged Show Auricula and veer to the accepted 1-2-4 proportions.

Blackpool Rock was one of three promising seedlings raised by the author in 1988 from a cross between 'Error', a blue-ground grey-edged Fancy, and 'Singer Stripe'. The range of colours which emerged from this pairing of genes was surprising, from black with white

Angel Eyes

stripes ('Königin der Nacht') through dark blue with white stripes ('Mrs. Davis') to 'Blackpool Rock' (pink with grey stripes). All three have a tendency to throw gawky scapes which spoil the balance of the plant. This is made worse as the pips may open much smaller than they should be. All three have lost vigour over the last twenty years and are not as easy to grow as when they were in their prime. None can be recommended for showing, though all three give a hint of what Stripes once were and may provide a different line in breeding. For display in your own collection, or for exhibition, look at some of the other varieties recommended in this list.

Blue Heaven is a strong grower with plenty of good features to please both experienced growers and those seeking just a pretty Stripe to grow for their own pleasure. Its well-mealed foliage provides a light background to set off the plentiful pips. These are of a dark blue with generous yet fine mealy stripes. The tube is a little pale but no more so than on any auricula carrying this type of colour, while the paste is as dense, gleaming and circular as anyone could wish. The periphery of the pips is also closer to a circle than many other Stripes (and Show Auriculas, for that matter). This is a reliable plant and should be considered amongst possible acquisitions.

Blush Baby is a recent entry on the auricula scene. It is notable for the smoother edge to the pips which are brightly striped with white farina over a shining red ground. Both tube and paste are also circular. The raiser thinks highly of this plant and grows it very well, putting fine plants on the showbench. Others have struggled to persuade it to grow vigorously. It is not uncommon for plants to behave in this way; even the most difficult varieties have endeavoured to please those who produced them. Be that as it may, Derek

Parsons' specimens are far too attractive to leave the plant in splendid isolation and, if you find an offset, try it, for it is a good variety and a really bright colour with a reasonably smooth outline.

Catherine Wheel is an early success from the Parsons' line of breeding and carries more than a hint as to the name of the raiser's wife. It stood out for the novelty of its colour which is a mixture of a copper-brown on which are stripes of yellow and grey meal. Edge and paste are quite good, though not up to the standard of later seedlings. It is not the easiest variety to grow, as the carrot can become coarse and rot and some trusses may reflex, but in the hands of a skilled grower, such as the raiser, it is a fine plant with real character. Should you come across an offset which likes your company, note that it gives a plentiful supply of viable pollen.

Cutie Pie is a reddish brown with pale yellow and white stripes. The tube and paste are good. Mr. Parsons recommends this variety as a parent which produces progeny of quality.

Catherine Wheel

Day By Day

Day By Day is a breakaway from the usual run of Stripes. The pips are larger than on many varieties and have a slightly smoother outline. At the centre of each is a round yellow tube surrounded by a solid white paste. From the outer edge of the paste stripes of yellow run out up the centre of each petal to the very periphery where there is a small notch. Surrounding the central yellow stripe are areas of a rich red which are flecked with smaller streaks of yellow. Small lines of farina are also scattered across the pip. A head of five or more blooms is a memorable sight.

Henry's Bane is one of a distinctive group of Parsons Stripes which catch the passing eye by dint of a green background. A closer examination of this plant reveals that the

Henry's Bane

green is genuinely green and no mere trompe l'oeuil. It is generously striped and splashed with a solid red and a few stripes and spots of farina. The extreme edge of each pip is finely outlined with a wire edge of red. The paste is not as round as on many others, the tube is a greenish yellow and the edge of the pips is nibbled, but the impact of this plant is considerable. It may not be a plant for the purist but it will find a place in many connections for its sheer impact.

Lemme Getatem is not the strongest variety amongst the Stripes. This is unfortunate as it is an attractive plant when in robust health. The underlying tissue of the blooms is pale but both tube and paste are round. The body is a pale off-white with mauve-blue streaks of colour running up the edges of the petals and adding little flecks of colour elsewhere too. The whole pip is sprinkled with meal.

Marion Tiger is the best of Allan Hawkes' numerous raisings and still one of the most shapely Stripes to be seen. It is not encountered at the shows as frequently as one might expect, given that it is a healthy plant with a reliable flowering habit and adequate offsets. Like many of the Allan Hawkes raisings, the basic colour is red on which are laid bright farinaceous stripes of grey and solid white. The tube is golden and round, surrounded by a good, bright paste, set off beautifully by the red beyond. The whole pip bears a cartilaginous ring at the edge of the petals which seems to hold back any potential raggedness normally associated with striping and lends a circularity to the pips. The mealy foliage further enhances the bold red of the truss. If you should have the opportunity to get hold of an offset, seize it. This is a plant for any collection.

Night and Day has all the looks of a delicate little thing but when shown with a truss of ten

Marion Tiger

Night and Day

111

pips it proves to be nothing of the sort. The underlying tissue of this variety is a very pale shade, a trait often connected with blue colouring right across the auricula clan. The tube carries a slightly raised rim which emphasises its roundness and is enhanced by neat anthers which cover the tube. The dense, white paste is equally circular and leads out into stripes of white tissue and white meal across the pale, lilac-blue ground. 'Night and Day' is popular with the leading growers and exhibitors and has already won many awards. This is a plant of quality and one you should seek out if you wish to grow Stripes.

Shining Hour is a remarkable creation. It is a robust grower with matt foliage, slightly crinkled at the edges. The blooms are of a type which Derek Parsons has developed recently. Their basic tissue appears for all the world as pale green, though a very close inspection reveals this to be cream with a tinge of green. From any other distance the eye does not take in the cream at all. The striping is a vivid red which contrasts sharply with the ground colour. The individual pips are nearer to a circular form than many Stripes.

Solero

Singer Stripe is one of Allan Hawkes' Stripes which derive their name from old brands of bicycle. It was very good at the time of its introduction in the 1980s but does not stand up so well to more recent varieties in competition. It is a deepish red in colour with grey or white stripes of farina. Given the right sort of mate, it is capable of throwing different colours in its offspring.

Solero is another of the surprises Tim Coop presented to us. It is a vigorous plant with nicely mealed foliage, throwing a strong scape on which it puts up good trusses of salmon coloured pips with broad stripes of white farina, a most attractive combination. Should you come across an offset, consider whether you want to grow Stripes for show or for personal enjoyment, for 'Solero' has won awards but it is not a classic for the showbench. The salmon body tends to appear as a broad band down the centre of each petal with the meal coalescing to form broad stripes up the petal edges. Though there are radial lines of farina up and down the body colour, the strictest of judges may consider it a failed edged type. If you know the judges' views on this in advance, you could always stage 'Solero'

Shining Hour

amongst the Fancies where it is bound to make an impact not only because of its bright combination of colours but also because of the round tube and excellent paste.

Stardust is amongst the best of the new Stripes. It is still showing the enthusiasm of youth, producing brightly mealed leaves to enhance the colours of its blooms. A truss of some seven or eight pips is calculated to stop many a spectator in their progress in order to wonder at the flowers. The tube is smooth and round with a slightly narrow but circular paste from which emanate broad white spokes of farina to set off the brilliant raspberry red of the ground. The edge is slightly uneven, but the whole pip is rounder than most of this kind. This is a beautiful plant.

Starsand is a personal favourite of the author, though not quite so highly regarded by the raiser who holds some of his more recent seedlings in higher esteem. It is not quite as vigorous as when absolutely new but it still grows well and throws attractive blooms of bright blue with delightful, white, farinaceous stripes. The blooms may reflex, given time and warmth, and they may have a ragged edge, but they are still a pleasure to see as they start to open. The brightly mealed foliage enhances the overall aspect of this plant. It may flower too early for some of the major shows, but it is such a comely plant that it is worth growing just for itself. When growing for competition, stake this one early.

The Argylls is probably the most shapely Stripe currently in existence. It is also, unfortunately, an extremely difficult individual and rare, as it shows no great desire to allow itself to be propagated. Once glimpsed, however, it remains a sight to remember. Its blooms are rounder than most other Stripes with a neat, round, golden tube and a solid, round, white paste surrounding it. The ground colour is a shining crimson with finely

laid stripes of white farina radiating out to the edge of each petal. The whole bloom carries a fine wire edge of farina in the best tradition of farina-bearing auriculas. One can but hope that a way will be found to allow this plant to become more widely available, as it is generally held to be the best of the whole tribe of Stripes at the moment.

Wye Hen is a startling change from the majority of the Parsons seedlings. The tissue underlying each bloom is a rich dark yellow which shows clearly at the top of the smooth, quite round tube. The paste is a good solid white and again quite round. The ground colour is a lovely orange-brown with good full-length radial stripes of farina. The rim of each petal also carries a thin line of the same farina. Plants of 'Wye Hen' always stand out on the showbench and attract great attention. The irony here is that this is one of the few plants which the raiser admits sometimes perform better in the hands of others than in his own – a rare occurrence indeed, but a typical piece of honesty on the part of Mr. Parsons.

Wye Hen

The New Striped Doubles From Derek Salt

The plants listed below are not widely available and may not become accessible to all. They are included to show the wide range of possibilities which the flowers may offer us if we seek carefully and assiduously. They will meet with enthusiastic approval from most florists and a more conservative reservation from others. They are of a form and colouring which has never been known amongst auriculas. We must hope that they fire the enthusiasm of other breeders to come up with similar achievements.

Greensleeves

Lincoln Clown

Greensleeves is one of a number of Doubles with a green base. The pips are attractively striped with both a meal and a darker green. The tube is well covered and the central petals nicely arranged.

Lincoln Clown bears a close resemblance to other modern Doubles in the formation of its prettily quartered pips, but the brownish yellow of each one is tinged and striped with maroon accompanied by fine farinaceous stripes. The meal is clearly visible around the rim of the central petals.

Lincoln Cuckoo is a paler shade of green than 'Greensleeves'. The striping is more muted in this variety, the whole truss having a cool, gentle aspect.

Lincoln Gemini is a striking plant. Its underlying tissue is a green shade of cream on which lie stripes of purple as the blooms begin to open and taking on a deep lilac shade as they fully unfold. The stripes themselves are streaked with smaller lines of the basic green-cream. Meal appears on the reverse of the petals, round the periphery of each and in stripes up and down each one. A potentially contentious point arises as the pips mature. The received view is that all pips in the truss should be uniform. The lilac at the part of the blooms which lies closest to the centre of the truss on Lincoln Gemini becomes lighter as the pips mature.

Lincoln Cuckoo

Lincoln Jester

Lincoln Gemini

Lincoln Melody

While this leaves two variations of the lilac colouring on pips, each pip behaves in the same way and at about the same time. The colouring is therefore uniform. Time and wise judges will form opinions on this but to the author's eye this is a very fine and very attractive plant. While scarce at the time of publication, one can but hope that it will bulk up quickly.

Lincoln Jester lives up to its name. The greenish yellow of the underlying tissue is clearly marked by stripes and splashes of bright purple and white meal. This is an eye-catcher, though still not easy to cultivate.

Lincoln Melody displays perhaps the boldest markings of any in this group. The ground is a dusky cream with vivid maroon stripes and a generous helping of mealy stripes to add to the whole confection.

Chapter 5
BORDER AURICULAS

Charles Rennie

The Borders are the quiet members of the auricula tribe. They do not have the more extrovert character of the exhibition types, coming in mainly muted shades. They will grow and thrive in any garden border which has just enough depth of reasonable soil and moisture. Acidity and alkalinity do not appear to have any effect on them, though the threat of a peaty bog or a lump of solid chalk might induce them to think otherwise. If your soil is open and not susceptible to standing in water, they should thrive. They prefer a position which gets some sun but does not expose them to too much heat. Some will even grow in quite a shady spot, provided that they receive enough light to permit them to recharge their batteries each day.

You may have just such a haven for them without realising it. You may have a shrub which acquires its foliage late or whose branches are not dense enough to cast total shade when in full leaf. Some fuchsias and smaller growing roses are ideal for this. An evergreen may also offer a position on the periphery of its space. If its branches wave to and fro in a breeze, it may just permit a Border Auricula to receive adequate light without becoming too hot.

Traditionally, this type of auricula was to be found lining the path leading up to the front door of some old, Victorian terraced houses. Sturdy clumps could be seen putting up their cheerful faces in April before the brighter colours of the annual flowers took over the display later in the season.

While it is possible to grow some of the sturdier Alpines or even some Show Auriculas in the garden border, they are sometimes susceptible to marking by bad weather. The farina on any Show variety will be spoilt by even a single drop of rain, leaving a very unattractive, white tear drop running down its glowing cheeks. Sturdy Alpines will often put up a good show for a number of years but they have been selected for their showbench performance when grown on a single stem. They may become too tall or clump up into a disproportionate mass of stems to look attractive for more than two or three years. While the true Borders do appreciate some splitting (and you may need to do this if your neighbours catch sight of them while blooming in spring), they usually have a convenient habit of sending out their stems sideways and then putting up new leaves at the eyes along these stems, so forming neat clumps. It is only when the older tissue at the heart of the clump begins to become too hard to prosper and shows signs of rot that you need to split them up.

Magnolia

Chamois

Border Bandit

While many seed-raised plants from market stalls and garden centres will prove adept at coping with the open garden, some old varieties continue to survive and thrive. These have been enjoyed by many generations of gardeners and should continue to provide similar pleasure into the foreseeable future. Newer plants are also emerging as their supporters hybridise the best of the current sorts, while occasional finds either from old gardens or from commercial sources are also introduced.

Classes specifically for Border Auriculas exist at all the major shows, thus bringing the plants to a wider public. Though few specific criteria exist for judging them in competition, it is generally agreed that a good Border Auricula should have a minimum of about three trusses of bloom and these should not be supported, thus displaying the plants as they would grow in the open garden. A large pan of fresh blooms with a compact habit and a sweet scent is a joy on show day for those with fond memories or just a sore back.

One advantage of the Border group is that they may enjoy the outdoor life for much of the year and be potted up in late winter or early spring, should you wish to exhibit a particularly attractive plant. After examining the roots for any signs of damage or insect pests, any dubious bits should be removed and pests treated with a suitable remedy. The foliage and stems should be thoroughly checked for any pests and similar measures taken to ensure the continued good health of your treasure. The plant should then be potted up in a pot or pan just wide and deep enough to accommodate the root ball. The potting compost may be of the type used for any auricula. Pour or spoon the soil around the

Schaumburg

Sonia Nicolle

roots, tapping the base of the pot gently on a flat surface periodically to ensure that it percolates down through all the spaces to the very bottom. Top dress the surface of the compost with a layer of grit to keep it moist and to present a tidier face to the world before plunging the pot or pan into a bowl or bucket containing just enough water to come up to the outer rim of your pot. It will soon make its way to the very top and dampen the surface. At this point you should remove the freshly potted plant from the water and place it in a cool place to drain. No particular attention should be needed before show day. Just make sure that the plant does not want for water or light and that it does not become too hot.

It is difficult to name all the varieties you might consider. Any good nursery catalogue will offer a sound selection of old and new. A few suggestions are give below:

Bellamy Pride	pearlescent white, vigorous; Best Plant in Show for Viv Pugh in 2009 at the Midlands and West Show
Bingley Folk	white
Blue Velvet	blue
Border Bandit	a recent introduction in a very pretty shade of soft orange
Broadwell Gold	sturdy, bright yellow; reminiscent of the wild *Primula auricula* but much more vigorous
Brownie	reddish brown; grown by Christopher Lloyd
Chamois	pale yellow brown; well named by its raiser, John Mercer, an expert grower of primulas
Charles Rennie	pink
Dales Red	black shading to red with a white paste at the centre
George Swinford's Leathercoat	pink to beige; believed to be a very old variety
McWatt's Blue	shades of blue and purple; scented
Old Irish Blue	deep blue
Old Red Dusty Miller	brick red to deeper red
Old Yellow Dusty Miller	yellow with a small mealy eye
Osborne Green	purple, green and cream
Rufus	bright brick red; may also be grown as a European hybrid
Silas	gold
Sonia Nicolle	cream and purple; from the former holder of the National Collection
The General	bright red
Windward Blue	pretty, pale blue
Winifred	brown and yellow

Chapter 6
EXHIBITING

Many new growers encounter auriculas at a show of some sort, perhaps one of those organised by the National Auricula and Primula Society or a more general one such as the Spring Shows at Harrogate or Malvern or even at Chelsea. When confronted by pristine examples of very high quality, some are likely to wonder whether they will ever be able to reproduce this quality of bloom for themselves. Fortunately a good number do and ask themselves whether they should really take the plunge and put their own efforts on public view. The answer is an emphatic 'Yes'! Any new exhibitor will be welcomed at a show and will be offered support and guidance by the more experienced members. Once you have taken the first bold step, you will find a new little world opening up where plants become available which you might not have expected to acquire before and the bonhomie and banter of the exhibitors will extend to you. Seek assistance with your first efforts and ask for advice, but, above all, do it. Given a little humility and disappointment, you will soon find that many a novice grower can swiftly advance to those august ranks of open competition.

TYPES OF EXHIBITION AURICULA

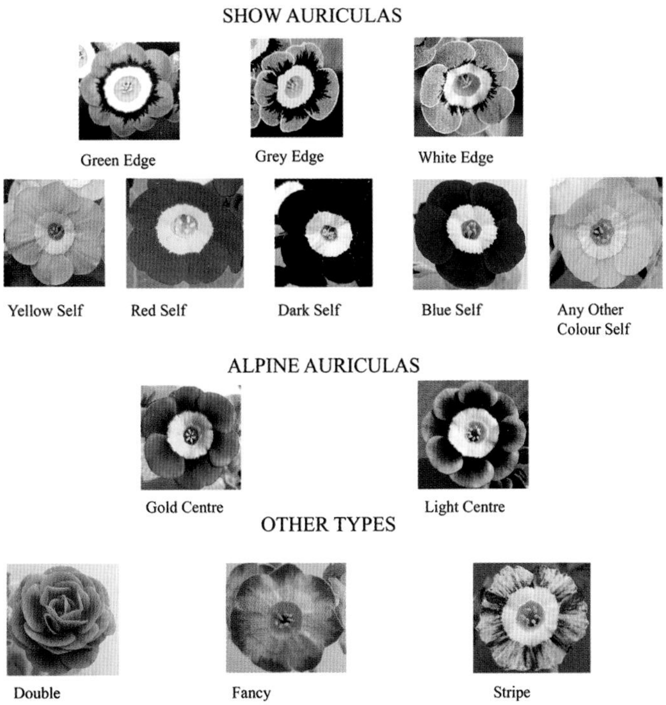

SHOW AURICULAS

Green Edge

Grey Edge

White Edge

Yellow Self

Red Self

Dark Self

Blue Self

Any Other Colour Self

ALPINE AURICULAS

Gold Centre

Light Centre

OTHER TYPES

Double

Fancy

Stripe

So how do you go about the task? Well, the first thing to do is consider how you prepare any auricula to show its best face to the world in a competition. Even if you do not take it anywhere near an exhibition hall, you may still provide yourself with a more attractive plant to enjoy in the privacy of your own greenhouse or frame. The neatest plants are those where a single crown (a single tuft of growth) is bearing its leaves and eventually its flowering stem. Make sure that it is in the centre of the pot and is growing upright. A little careful re-potting might be necessary to achieve this, but auriculas in full growth will tolerate the process. Re-potting may also be necessary if the carrot has grown too long and is protruding from the compost like a miniature palm tree. In such a case, carefully remove a little compost from the base of the root ball and drop the plant further down into a clean pot, covering up the lanky growth with fresh, open compost and water in gently. If the outside of the pot is at all dirty or encrusted, swap it for a clean one. The judges make their awards on the merits of the plants, but they might just be swayed in your direction if there are two plants of equal merit and yours looks cleaner. As soon as you have marked out a plant as potential exhibition material, take all precautions to ensure that the foliage stays clean. Mealed foliage marred by water splashes looks unsightly, as do fresh green leaves on meal-free types which are marked with compost or lime blotches from water. Should there be any leaks in the glazing of your greenhouse or frame, move the plant away from the spot where you know the water comes through. Now you must wait until the flowering scape begins to push upwards.

As soon as the scape allows you to see that it is carrying a good truss of bloom, provide some support. It will not need anything to carry any weight at the moment, but you can ensure that it grows straight up and does not lean sideways. It will also enable you to spot potential show specimens amongst your collection. Various forms of support have been employed over the years and there is no special type. The main thing is that it should not detract from the appearance of the plant when it is in full bloom by being either too long, too thick or of a garish colour. The commonest type of stake found at the national shows is a small piece of bamboo skewer, the type used for food preparation. This needs to go as close to the scape as possible. A little care may be needed in selecting the exact spot to insert the sharp point of the skewer. If you know that a main root emerges from the carrot at a particular point, move the skewer round a little. It is also awkward if you find that the very place where you wish to insert the stake is blocked by the junction of two leaves. A small measure of judicious manoeuvring or, if the worst comes to the worst, the removal of one leaf will usually enable you to find a suitable spot.

Once the stake is in place, you may care to cut off any excess, though make sure you have a good 7in. (18cm) showing above the compost. You may be surprised how much the scape can extend as the truss expands. Any excess can be cut away later. If you choose to trim when the pips are at their best it takes away any guesswork, but it is also not as easy to snip off the last piece of the support when it is surrounded by beautiful flowers. As growth progresses, the main stem of your flowering truss may wish to incline to one side. This is the time to offer it some gentle encouragement by pulling it into the support. Growers use various means to do this. The old favourite is a short length of green or a very light-colour wool, though any sort of soft cord will suffice. Loop it gently around the scape and cross the two ends of the tie before you feed them round the support. This gives a figure of 8, so leaving some of the tie as a cushion between the plant stem and the wood. If you now tie loosely at the rear of the support, the wool or cord should stay in place without restricting the growth of the

Top left: A soft tie goes round the scape

Top right: Pass the tie between the scape and the support before tying it behind the stake

Above left: Cut off the tie as neatly as possible

Above right: Insert cotton wool to space the pips if needed

flowering stem. If you find that your tie slips down the stake, simply circle it round the wood once more before tying a knot. The main pitfalls to avoid are cutting into the flesh of the scape or leaving an all too obvious tie. Remember, however, that any tie part way up the scape is best removed before taking the plant to the showbench, though you will sometimes find winning specimens with a tie halfway up the stem. Some judges ignore this,

but others regard it as a flaw if it spoils the neatness of the plant.

As the truss starts to grow, you will need to consider the number of pips your plant is capable of bearing and also the question of how many you will need for exhibition purposes. For some plants it is a physical possibility to carry more than a dozen pips over the flowering spell. If you just want the maximum quantity, you may care to let it have its own way, but for a good exhibition specimen you will need to cull a few buds. The first pip on some varieties can prove to be coarse and out of character, though this is not always the case. If you know this to apply to your plant, however, remove this king bud and allow the vigour to go into those which will come later. The last few pips in a truss also tend to be weaker than those that have enjoyed the plant's first burst of energy. They are frequently smaller and angular. Only experience can provide this information about each variety. As the truss develops, it is better to remove these last, weak buds and allow the plant to concentrate on the prime ones. An ideal pip traditionally has a diameter of about 1⅛in. (29-32mm), Selfs, Doubles and Alpines tending towards the lower end and Edges towards the upper end.

Make sure that you know the minimum number of pips a plant has to carry on show day before you remove any blooms. Make sure too that you have a finely pointed pair of scissors and a steady hand before you begin. It is not unknown for even the most respected exhibitors to inadvertently snip or pull off the wrong bud (or even the bulk of a truss) in trying to remove a single pip.

There are no rules as to the best number of pips to display but an odd number sometimes appeals to the eye more than an even number. It is not always the case but it can be no coincidence that the same principle applies when planting up a garden border.

If at all possible, try to coax at least one pip to fill any gap that may be left in the centre of the truss.

While a few, admirable auriculas have well-placed footstalks which send out their buds at nice, even spacing to produce a beautifully balanced, hemispherical head of bloom, most do not. It is left to the florist to persuade them. Unfortunately, imprecations and cursing have no effect whatsoever. Instead, the deployment of small blobs of cotton wool gently inserted between the footstalks usually persuade them to incline to one side or the other. You may even cross the footstalks over each other, if it helps the individual pips to be displayed more evenly. The aim is to allow the spectator to see an evenly spread head of bloom on which the pips just touch each other without overlapping and without great gaps between them. Bear in mind that this is perfection and is rarely seen, though many good approximations are arrived at each year. All the pips you put before the viewing public should be of the same

colouring and freshness, though again this is the aim and usually a small variation is permissible, since all the pips will never open together. Provided that they all look very similar, they will pass muster.

Meal occurring in inappropriate places on the pips is more likely on Show varieties than on present-day Alpines. In the past, speckles could be found on the eye of some Gold Centres but that is now infrequent, thanks to the diligence of those who breed them. Should you discover any, however, be sure to remove them before you put your plant on the bench. The favourite tool for this is a small, soft painting brush with which you may flick away the unwanted flecks, taking great care not to smear them any further across the face of the pip. Any soft implement with a reasonably narrow end might fulfil the same task. Cotton buds may perform the task but they need special care as they can also smudge the meal. Be sure to wipe the point of the bristles frequently in order to keep them clean.

Unwanted farina on the body of an edged variety or on a Self Show Auricula may pose a more challenging problem. The meal is in fact a small blob of wax set on top of a tiny hair. If you dislodge it and cause it to contact the coloured surface below, it will be very difficult to clean away. The most adroit of growers may accomplish the feat with a dry brush. An odd enthusiast my prefer to moisten the tip of the brush between his or her lips immediately before using it. Again, make sure you keep the point of the brush clean. The riskiest course of action is to use the tiniest amount of methylated spirit on the tip of the bristles and to just touch the undesired speck with it. The spirit will dissolve the wax. Should it touch the surface of the pip, it will leave a mark which cannot be removed. This particular method is one requiring a very steady hand and some considerable practice before use in a critical situation. If in doubt, don't meddle.

Some Green Edges will put up their pips with a fine line of meal round the very rim of their petals. This is known as a China edge. Although not a terrible fault, you may wish to remove it. Again, a dry brush applied carefully may do the job. The growers of old sometimes used milk to achieve their aim. It is a remedy I have never tried and is rarely encountered. If you are unsure about what to do, leave it and talk it over with other enthusiasts who may help you to find a method which you find convenient. It is better in the meantime to display a plant with a minor fault than no plant at all.

The ideal plant should have a single crown from which the leaves and the blooms emerge. Sometimes this is not possible. You may want to keep all the offsets which are just appearing round the collar of your prize specimen if this is your sole example of this variety or if this one is looking particularly sturdy. In such a case there is little to be done other than to hope that the plant does not look too untidy or that the truss of bloom is so good that the judges will disregard the remainder of the plant. If you need some offsets but not necessarily all of them, remove those which look as though they have a few roots and pot them up; remove also those which are very small and may not prove to be sufficiently sturdy. One or two offsets like this may not mar too much the overall appearance of the plant. If you do have adequate offsets of a particular plant, remove those on your proposed exhibit to leave the single crown.

For many newcomers to the showbench (and sometimes for the older hands too), a heart-rending decision must sometimes be taken if a plant has a new offset which is also beginning to throw a flower stem. The grower must now consult the rules for a particular show. Usually you will find wording such as 'Secondary trusses should be neatly tied down'. This means that you will need to insert a small stake somewhere near the rim of the pot and carefully bend down the new stem so that it does not impede a clear view of the main flower truss. If the judges decide that your plant is bearing superior blooms to its competitors, they will award your plant the appropriate prize. Should they consider that the flowers on another plant are the equal of yours and that the tied-down stem detracts from the overall appearance of your exhibit, the other plant will be given the prize card. You will find prize cards allotted to some exhibits with secondary stems of this type, but you will find more which have been passed over. Unless the second truss is absolutely essential, snip it off, no matter how much it grieves you at the time. You might even care to wear it as a buttonhole for the rest of the day to show what a good grower you are. It might depress your opponents.

If you now have a number of well-presented plants you would like to put on the showbench, you need to decide what the demands of the show require of you. If you have a single specimen of any particular type, you will find an appropriate section at any show, be it Edged, Self, Fancy, Stripe, Light Centre Alpine, Gold Centre Alpine or Double. If you have several which you think are more than ordinary, read the schedule and make certain you know in which classes your plants belong. You will find classes for a group of six, four, three or two plants staged as multi-pot exhibits. There are sometimes classes for a matched pair. Read the schedule carefully and, if you are not quite sure where your plants are best staged, ask either the Show Super-intendent, one of the stewards or another exhibitor. The former are there to ensure that the show runs smoothly for all exhibitors, while the old hands are almost without exception glad to help out a newcomer. Should you strike one of them at the busiest periods of the day, then he or she will usually take a little time out to point you towards someone with more time (and fewer plants) who will provide guidance.

In your reading of the schedule, check the exact wording for each class. If you have a group of four plants, does the wording stipulate that they all have to be of different varieties or are you allowed to show four plants but your group must contain at least three different varieties? In the case of the latter, you may show two plants of a particular variety and two others, each of different varieties. If you are showing Alpines, check whether the wording for the class stipulates Gold or Light Centres. Sometimes you are required to show one Light and one Gold, while in other places you are required to put up two plants with the same coloured centre. A matched pair means that you have to stage two plants not just of the same general type but of the same named variety and looking very similar to each other. Take note too of the minimum number of pips required and make sure you have at least that number.

When you have sorted out the classes in which your plants may belong, have a close look at them and try to make them fit in with each other so that in the multi-pot classes each one enhances its neighbour. First of all, look at the height of the flowering scapes. You have to place your pots on the showbench in a row, one behind the other. You may like the look of two particular ones which seem to complement each other nicely, but do they vary too much in height? A slight slope down in the heights of the plants from the back to the front of your group is a very frequent arrangement, but to have, for instance, a tall Blue Self at the back of a group of three, a short Grey Edge before it with a tall Red Self at the front would create a dip in the centre of the three. If these were your only possibilities for a group of three, arrange them with the taller of the two Selfs at the rear, the shorter Self in the centre with the Grey at the front. You might also consider splitting them up and putting two of the three in a class for two plants and the third in a class for one plant. A very even (and more difficult) arrangement is to find three plants of about the same height. The majority of judges look more favourably on a group across which (in the words of the old Lancashire judges) 'you could place a board'.

When you have decided on your grouping, remove any packing from between your pips and very carefully remove any unopened buds. The packing would bring about a disqualification and the unopened buds are counted as a fault, since the judges look only for perfect pips. Make sure that you have written out the appropriate label for your plant and that it does not detract from the overall appearance and then carefully ferry your potential prize-winners to the appropriate class. You may need to make two or more journeys to accomplish this, but do not rush. You have spent a lot of time in getting everything ready and it would be a waste to dash through a doorway only to find your treasure crushed against the jacket of a fellow competitor coming in the opposite direction. Keep a record of which plants you have put in each class to help you to collect all of them at the end of the show. Every year one or two are left behind on the benches and, while most of them can be recognised from the exhibitor's number on the plant ticket, there are always odd ones which seem to have been abandoned.

The rest of the day should now consist of a little suspense, while the judges make their tour of the tables, some lunch and a good day's comparing of notes with other exhibitors. If you are new to the craft, you may even seek advice from one of the judges as to how to improve your exhibits, but do not head towards them to pour out a tirade of criticism. They will have been associated with auriculas for a long time and are selected for their knowledge, experience and sharp eye. Most are willing to assist and, should you be unfortunate enough to come across one who is not, seek out another who will. With their help you may have an even more successful day the following spring.

Class for four combined auriculas.

A List of Plants Described in the Text
Arranged in Exhibition Categories

ALPINE – GOLD
CENTRE

Ancient Society
Applecross
Bilbo Baggins
Blossom
Blyth Spirit
Bolero
Finchfield
Gary Pallister
Gay Crusader
Goldthorn
Landy
Largo
Lee Paul
Merridale
Nickity
Piers Telford
Prince John
Rodeo
Sandwood Bay
Sirius
Sonny Boy
Sumo
The Lady of the Vale
Toffee Crisp
Vera

ALPINE – LIGHT
CENTRE

Andy Cole
Avril
Blue Yodeler
C.W. Needham
Dilly Dilly
Divint Dunch

Frank Crosland
Gordon Douglas
Highland Park
Ian Greville
John Wayne
Joy
Kevin Keegan
Langley Park
Mark
Mehta
Pequod
Quarry Lane
Rowena
Sandra
Sophie
Spartan
Stella North
Stella South
Victoria de Wemyss
Walton

SHOW – GREEN EDGE

Beechen Green
Benny Green
Bob Lancashire
Chloë
Figaro
Fleminghouse
Grüner Veltliner
Haffner
Hew Dalrymple
Jack Wood
Julia
Jupiter
Moselle
Orb
Paris

Perdito/Perdita
Prague
Prosperine
Roberto
Sappho
Scipio
Serenity
Tamino
The Mekon

SHOW – GREY EDGE

Clare
Corporal Jones
Galatea
Gavin Ward
Grey Hawk
Iago
Lovebird
Margaret Martin
Orlando
Pikey
Sergeant Wilson
St. Boswells
Teem
Warwick

SHOW – WHITE EDGE

Brookfield
Douglas White
Godfrey
James Arnot
Michael Wattam
Minstrel
Ptarmigan
Sharmans Cross
Snowy Owl

The Bride
Walhampton
White Satin
White Wings

SHOW SELF
(Shown in brackets are the
exhibition categories into
which each plant falls)

April Moon (Yellow)
Barbarella (Dark)
Blue Jean (Blue)
Blue Cliff (Blue)
Blue Steel (AOC)
Brasso (Yellow)
Brompton (Yellow)
Chanel (AOC)
Cheyenne (Red)
Chiffon (AOC)
Corntime (Yellow)
Derwentwater (AOC)
Eaton Dawn (AOC)
Geronimo (Red)
Gizabroon (Dark)
Jac (Blue)
Joel (Blue/AOC)
Kiowa (Red)
Knights (Red)
Lavenham (AOC)
Limelight (AOC)
Miss Otis (AOC)
Moonglow (AOC)
Neat and Tidy (Dark)
Nocturne (Dark)
Oakes Blue (Blue)
Prince Bishops (Blue)
Royal Mail (Red)
Scorcher (Red)
Sharon Louise (Yellow)
Sherbet Lemon (Yellow)
Super Para (Dark)

Taffeta (AOC)
The Mikado (Dark)
Upton Belle (Yellow)
Watchet (AOC)
Whistlejacket (AOC)
Wincha (Dark)
Windermere (AOC)

FANCY

Blue Chip
Coffee
Conservative
Crimple
Crinoline
Denim
Fanfare
Green Café
Green Mustard
Hawkwood
Hinton Fields
Hot Lips
Minley
Moon Fairy
Rag Doll
Rajah
Space Age
Spring Meadows
Star Wars
Sweet Pastures

DOUBLE

Brimstone and Treacle
Buttermere
Cameo Beauty
Chiquita
Corrie Files
Crimson Glow
Doyen
Fred Booley
Funny Valentine

Golden Hind
Jane Myers
Kentucky Blues
Lincoln Bullion
Lincoln Chestnut
Marigold
Mary
Matthew Yates
Metis
Mipsie Miranda
Paphos
Prima
Reynardyne
Samantha
Sarah Gisby
Stripey
Susannah
Sword
Trouble
William Gunn

STRIPES

Angel Eyes
Bittersweet
Blue Heaven
Blush Baby
Catherine Wheel
Cutie Pie
Day by Day
Henry's Bane
Lemme Getatem
Marion Tiger
Night and Day
Shining Hour
Singer Stripe
Solero
Stardust
Starsand
The Argylls
Wye Hen

Chapter 7
JUDGING

Most show flowers have a scale of points which the judges award to various characteristics of a flower. A number of scales for auriculas have been put forward in the past. Unfortunately, they require a point score to be given to individual parts of the plant. Since no two pips on an auricula truss are identical, to do so at a show would be very time-consuming. Some also pre-suppose that the maximum points allotted to each part of the plant are the same. Since there has always been disagreement amongst the leading growers as to which are the most important features of a plant and which are the gravest faults, no such system has ever been put into practice effectively. All may be valuable in the confines of an individual greenhouse or frame, especially when you wish to assess a seedling, but they are both too vague and therefore too clumsy to be of value on show day. Just imagine the time it would need to effect the task in the class for six Alpines if each plant had six pips, if there were six plants in each exhibit and if there were six sets of plants.

The judges are selected by the National Auricula and Primula Society's officers because of their knowledge and experience. They talk to the foremost growers and breeders and publish their own views in the year books of the three sections. Should it be deemed that they are failing to represent the views of those who are staging the plants, the Society simply invites someone else to act as judge. On show day the judges have to make many evaluations based on their own knowledge and experience. If you disagree with the judges' decision, just ask them quietly why they opted for any particular plant in favour of another. They will usually find time to explain what caught their eye. They will always have reasons; it is never as naïve as

'because I liked it'. Subjectivity and personal preferences are left behind as soon as the show superintendent asks everyone to leave the hall and announces that the judging will now begin. The standards on which the judges base any decisions are published by each Section of the National Society. These in turn go back largely to the first half of the nineteenth century or even earlier. They contain the wisdom of writers such as James Maddock and George Glenny but are couched mainly in a more modern style.

The judges carry in their heads an idea of what they expect from any plant or set of plants. On occasions they may consider that the standard expected for a particular award has not been reached. When this happens, they may decide not to allot a prize to an exhibit. This happens most frequently in a bad year when the standard of the plants is below par. The judges may then award second and third prizes but no first, since they consider that a first prize should only go to a good exhibit. This is not popular at times, the argument being made that some exhibit must be the best on the day. When the judges withhold awards, they are seeking to continue the standard of the plants from one year to the next.

THE INITIAL CHECKS
The judges' first task on approaching the bench is to check the specification for the class. If it is a group of Selfs, for example, they will make sure that there are no edged plants present. They will then count the number of entries and plants. It is not unknown for the pressure of staging to cause even experienced exhibitors to put their plants in the wrong class, a pair in a three-pot class for example. In multi-pot classes, the judges check that the exhibits conform to specification. If the

schedule stipulates a minimum number of varieties, that also has to be checked. This is a task which can be undertaken en bloc at the start or individually as each exhibit is looked over. Only when these necessary preliminaries are gone through can the assessment of the plants begin.

GENERAL APPEARANCE AND CONDITION

So, what are the judges going to consider? First of all they will have a look at the general condition of the plants. Freshness is the prime consideration here. If the plants look bright, brisk and healthy, then the foliage should show the appropriate degree of stiffness and the shade of grey, green or white which characterises a particular type. It should not be over-long or lax. Prior to staging your plants, make sure that no little visitors such as aphids have taken up residence. A vigorous plant will have sufficient width of leaves to cover the top of the pot. Two centuries ago, a leaf or two standing up behind the truss was considered to enhance the pips. Nowadays, the judges look for a modest length of scape extending clear of the foliage. Given that the overall length of the stem should be about 4in.-7in. (10cm-18cm), the leaves should not become drawn. They look out of place if they reach up to the lower edge of the blooms and, if they then flop over the top of the compost, leave the plant looking sad and weary.

If a plant with mealy leaves is exhibited, the farina should be as pristine as possible. Given that water has to be applied to the plants and that some jolting will take place when you transport the plants, this is by no means easy. In the case of green leaves, there must be no marks from water, sprays or farina from the mealy types on them.

If a stake is needed to support a stem, it must be kept as unobtrusive as possible. Whether it is made of cane or wire, is green or white, is tied with wool or cord, is immaterial provided that it does not mar the aspect of the stem or truss. Perfection is a straight scape of appropriate length, strong enough to hold the truss above the leaves without a stake. No grower should be tempted to use any supporting material to do anything other than keep the scape upright. Any suspicion that it might be propping up the pedicels or the pips could lead to a disqualification. This will also follow if you leave any packing between the pips.

An ideal plant should have a single rosette of leaves. Most vigorous varieties will, however, try to throw offsets. The judges will not necessarily downpoint a plant with an offset still attached but, all other things being equal, they may prefer one with a single crown.

A problem arises when a plant throws a second truss of bloom. The rules permit this to be tied down neatly using a pin or small stake. The judges will always judge the truss which the exhibitor has presented, but, once again, if two plants are in close contention, the neater, more symmetrical presentation will be preferred.

The pots in which you stage your plants should conform to the specifications laid down by the show rules. They should not play a great part in the judging of a plant except in those odd cases of very close competition, but do make sure that they are clean. Dirty pots will obviously not impress the judges. Above all, make sure that you give your pots a wipe before they go on the bench. It is unpleasant to handle a dirty, slimy pot and odd instances have occurred where such an item has slipped from a judge's fingers.

SOME FAULTS IN SHOW AURICULAS

STIGMA VISIBLE ABOVE ANTHERS

MEAL ON THE BODY

CUTS IN PASTE

CRENATED TUBE

BREAK IN BODY COLOUR

POINTED PETALS

CRACKS IN PASTE

ANGULAR PASTE

DOUBLE WIDTH PETAL

FLASHING UP THE EDGE

At this point, the judges will begin to consider the blooms. Let us think again about the parts of the auricula bloom. In the Edged group they are the tube, the paste, the ground or body colour and the edge. If the edge carries no farina, the plant is said to be a Green Edge. If there is a light coating of meal, it is a Grey Edge. If the meal is particularly dense, it will cover the underlying tissue so thickly that it appears white and is classified as a White Edge. Selfs have no edge; their colour extends out to the rim of the pip without shading. Alpines have no paste; they have an eye of a light or golden colouring and their body shades out from a dark colour near the eye to a lighter version of the same near the periphery. Stripes have a paste or an eye and have stripes which run out like spokes in a wheel towards the rim. Let us have a look at each type individually.

EDGED SHOW AURICULAS

THE TUBE

At the centre of all exhibition auriculas is the tube which holds the reproductive organs, the anthers which carry the pollen and the pistil with the stigma on top which takes the pollen down to fertilise the ovules at the bottom. The stigma has to be tucked away, well and truly out of sight. If it stands above or between the anthers, the judges will disqualify the plant. Pin-eyed plants are plain for all to see, with the stigma at the top of the tube and the anthers below it at the base. These are never seen on the showbench. Occasionally a rogue plant crops up where the anthers sit approximately at the top of the tube but the pistil extends so far up the tube that the stigma sits amongst them. If we are to maintain the standards handed down, a plant of this type must be deemed inadmissible.

The anthers themselves should be fresh and bright. Any plant with newly emerged pollen stands out. Even if the anthers have already burst, a good quantity of pollen is an attractive feature. A few varieties produce little pollen. Provided that the anthers open sufficiently to provide some covering for the tube, the flower may still pass muster.

When the judges come to the tube, however, things are less straightforward. The tube should be a bright gold to set off the rest of the pip. Unfortunately, even the brightest golden tubes can become less brilliant with age. If it is possible, remove any pip where the colour has become dingy; otherwise be prepared for some downgrading of the truss. The colour of the tube also varies between varieties. Some are paler than others. No matter how good the rest of the pip may be, if the tube lacks brilliance, it puts the plant at a disadvantage. Some latitude is given here to Blue Selfs. The auricula tribe seems to show blue colouring only on pale underlying tissue. Some blues open quite bright in the tube but soon fade. Provided that the tube does not fade to the point of translucency with a blue type, the judges will exercise some discretion.

The shape of the tube has long been a source of some contention. 'Round' is the term traditionally applied to it. The trouble is that the rim of the tube may be simple and circular — rather as if someone has drawn it with a pair of compasses — or its periphery may have a tiny frill which looks like the edge of a sea shell. 'Teem' and many of its descendants such as 'Margaret Martin' show this latter feature. Both types have been accepted, mainly, I suspect, because some of the varieties displaying these crenations have otherwise been so good. If circularity is one of our criteria, however, the indentations should be regarded as a fault.

The width of the tube and its relationship to the rest of the corolla has been a matter for discussion — usually amicable — for more than two hundred years. The debate turned round the question of how much of the corolla the tube, the paste, the body and the edge should each occupy. Two schools of thought have evolved, though auriculas are disinclined to adhere strictly to either. The earliest florists decided that the form which most appealed to their eye was one in which the tube occupied one sixth of the width of the pip. The outer edge of the paste beyond this then extended to one half of the pip's diameter. The remaining area was taken up by the body and the edge in about equal measures. This scheme was set out by Maddock in 1792, as we saw in Chapter 1.

A slightly different set of proportions was proposed by George Glenny who began writing about show plants from the 1830s. Whereas Maddock supported the above proportions of 1:3:6 for tube, paste and body plus edge, Glenny preferred 1:2:4. This means that, while the width of the body plus edge remains constant under both schemes, in Glenny's the tube is broader and the width of the paste is reduced. We cannot know for certain why the two theorists came up with different views. It has been said that a narrow tube is harder to breed. It has also been countered that a wider tube permits more of the golden colour at the centre. A further complication is that a broader tube will also permit the stigma to be seen more easily, thus leaving the plant open to severe down-pointing or disqualification. If you look at some modern Green Edges such as 'Chloë' and its close descendants, you will see the 1:2:4 proportions with a wide tube, but, just below the anthers, a small platform with a gap at the centre constricts the cylinder. It looks for all the world as though the anthers are fixed round the edge of a small, light yellow cup. It may be that a cup of this type had come about by Glenny's time and the growers thought that this added an improved, bright contrast to the flower. Glenny also mentions that the edge of the tube should rise a trifle above the paste. This feature seems to have declined until it began to stage a resurgence quite recently. It is nowadays met occasionally in the 1:3:6 types where it adds an extra hint of gold to the tube.

These standards for the tube refer to Edged and Self varieties of Show Auricula. One difficulty, already commented on, remains: that is the colour of the tube in Show Auriculas where the body contains any hint of blue. In his monograph on the auricula, Sir Rowland Biffen,

an eminent scientist who died in 1949, explained that the pigment which gives auriculas their colour produces different results depending on the alkalinity or acidity of the cell sap of the plant. If the sap is acid, the bloom will tend towards red. If it is alkaline, the colour will lean towards the blue side. If we think about Alpine Auriculas, the blue shades crop up amongst the Light Centres (with their lighter coloured eye and tube), while the bright red shades are met with in the Gold Centres (with golden tubes). True, some shades of red occur in the Light Centres, but these are always of a wine to pale rose persuasion and never show the fiery colours of many Gold Centres. Could it be that the alkalinity of the cell sap also leads the blue shades in Show Auriculas? Certainly, no modern Blue Selfs are blessed with a golden tube. Some varieties open quite a decent shade of lemon (a colour, incidentally, which Glenny deemed acceptable) but fade as the pip matures. On the showbench a certain latitude is shown, as we have commented, towards the Blue Selfs in this regard.

But what are we to make of the rising number of Edged Auriculas with a blue ground? Here there is no dispensation in the tradition. As yet we have no such varieties with any claim to real form which also possess the constitution to go on from year to year. I have no doubt that they will emerge. Should that happen, we would have to re-think their appropriate place on the bench. Either we create a separate class for them or we follow Glenny's advice on the acceptability of a lemon tube. For the time being, any prospective exhibitor should be aware that the tradition asks for a golden tube.

THE PASTE

There are no such problems when we come to examine the paste. It should extend from the rim of the tube to about halfway across the disc of the corolla. It must be white, dense, even, smooth and round. The whiteness of the paste is eye-catching. If you are new to showing auriculas, beware of a few varieties where there is a tinge of cream in the white. This could be the case with one or two of the old-timers amongst the White Edges. Put one of these next to a good white paste and the contrast becomes clear. Nearly all recent introductions are also free of the granular paste which used to be met with. A close examination of such a type will reveal tiny snowballs of paste instead of the smoothness of potato flour which the judges expect. Occasionally the paste will become thin and crack. A plant with this fault should be left in the greenhouse. So should any where an insect has landed and wiped its feet either directly on the paste or has picked up farina from the paste and marked the body or petals with it.

The periphery of the paste can be problematical. If an exhibitor is tempted to stage a variety with a hint of yellow either at the petal joins or running round the outermost edge of the paste, he or she should think again. The judges will not look favourably on it. They will also reject any plant where the paste is angular. This fault crops up frequently on blooms with five petals but it is also found on those with more. The annoying thing about this defect is that it may occur on the later pips of a plant where the earlier ones were perfectly good. Where this happens, the exhibitor may want to stage the plant in a difficult year. It is unlikely to gain the winner's red card, but it is always better to have a few plants to look at in a truly bad time. The last fault is the most difficult. The perfect pip has a paste which extends to the bottom of the join between the petals. If that join is too long, it will cut the edge of the paste. Unfortunately, many varieties carry this fault. The worst thing that can happen is for the two petals on either side of the join to be at different heights, so emphasising the crack. A perfect paste is a rare occurrence. The judges know about it and understand, but they will still pursue perfection, knowing that it is rare to find it.

THE GROUND OR BODY COLOUR

The body colour or ground surrounds the paste. It is usually black but it may be any colour. Whatever colour it displays, it must be bright, solid and not shaded. We have already mentioned the danger of a line of yellow where the paste meets the body but the judges will not countenance a similar line where the body meets the green, grey or white edge. What they will look for in this last place is the least formal aspect of a very formal flower. This is the feathering of the ground into the green, grey or white of the edge. This outer rim of the body should form tiny streaks of colour which run like flames into the outer tissue. They should be evenly distributed and should not run out to the rim of the pip. This fault occurs most commonly at the edge of the petals and is often referred to as 'flashing up the edge'. Most edged auriculas show this fault to some degree and it would be a great find if a variety were to emerge which was free from it. A fault not found in recent varieties is that of a scattering of meal on the body colour. Exhibitors who try to remove it should be aware that a smear or a trace of liquid used to remove the meal from the ground will show up and be faulted.

The last feature of the body colour to bear in mind is that of its width. In the nineteenth and early twentieth centuries, the body was usually as wide as the edge tissue. Around the middle of the twentieth century, there was a move towards a narrower ground. It may be that the extra width of the edge added a bit more brightness to the pips; it could just be that it was a novelty which still maintained the otherwise traditional appearance of the blooms. At times the ground was reduced to a fine line of dark colouring. In the last twenty years, the wider ground has staged something of a comeback and has again found favour with the growers. Because both have been accepted and neither rejected, the judges will approve any width which is sufficient to register a clear contrast with the edge but which does not dominate the pip or render it thunderously gloomy.

THE EDGE

The edge should now add the final touch of distinction to the unique formation of the auricula's blooms. In most cases it will be close in appearance to the foliage, though some Greys and Whites insist on putting more powder on the pips than on the leaves. If the edge is green, there must be no trace of farina on it. The edge tissue may be of any shade of green but it should form a satisfying contrast with the ground, paste and tube. Although the judges will accept darker shades of green, the lighter side of the spectrum often provides a bright touch. This has not always been the case. The growers of the first half of the twentieth century were all for the darker shades. This is an instance where the tradition is altering with tastes swinging towards a different view and yet not ruling out the older one. A line of meal exists on the very rim of some Green Edges which is traditionally referred to as a China edge. It has found favour with some enthusiasts but it is considered a fault by judges generally. Green really should mean green.

If the edge is grey, its underlying green tissue should be moderately dotted with particles of meal. These should be evenly distributed on the edge but must not stray on to the body. The density of the particles varies from one variety to another but should be constant on all the pips on a truss which the exhibitor presents to the judges. The whiteness of this farina and the shade of green inherent in the underlying tissue combine to give an individual quality of greyness to each variety. When the meal on the edge is very dense, the green tissue of the edge will not be immediately obvious amongst the farina. Any plant of this type is a White Edge. The judges will look for a clear shade of white and will fault anything which might appear cream or dingy, a criticism which could be levelled at some of the older White Edges. Great care is needed in handling plants with farinose edges. Any smearing will be considered a defect.

With edged plants of any type, the judges will fault a plant where the edge cuts through the body colour and touches the paste.

THE PIP IN GENERAL

The petals of the pip should form a shape as near to a circle as possible. They should be equal to each other in size, so giving an appearance of evenness to the pip. Petals which are twice the width of the others (an all too common fault) are a weakness. The petals should have a smooth edge without notches, and the indentations at the joins of the petals should not detract from the overall roundness of the pip. Flatness is the other demand of each pip. It too is an elusive quality in most edged varieties. If some petals should open cupped, it is possible to curl them gently to flatten them out, but great care and patience is needed. Cockled pips will, however, count as a fault.

These are the ideals which the judges will look for. Every now and then a perfect pip or two will be presented but it is indeed a rare treat to find anything like this. Given the complex genetic make-up of the Edged Auricula, this is not surprising and the judges are aware of the problems but they will go on looking for perfection amongst all the offerings. The size of the pips is generally reckoned to be at its best with a diameter of about 1¼in. (32mm). The judges don't walk around with a ruler or any form of template; they know from experience when a pip is in character. One or two varieties try to throw overblown blooms which do not become the rest of the plant. The fault is emphasised when the scape is of an ordinary length, for then the excessive size of the pips will spoil the proportions of the exhibit. Pips which are smaller than their neighbours will also detract from the overall good looks of the truss. You will notice that these tend to have an angular paste. Remove any offenders, since the tradition of the auricula is that only good pips should be shown. Unopened buds and imperfect blooms are regarded as faults.

One vexed question raised with exhibition auricula blooms is whether to dress the petals. This is a technique employed by skilled exhibitors of Alpine Auriculas. The natural state of the vast majority of auriculas is to open their blooms with some petals lying over the edge of their neighbour. By nature they do not do this in an organised fashion, leaving the right-hand edge of each petal overlying the left-hand side of its neighbour, for example. Instead some will overlap a part of a neighbour on one side, while another will choose to cover the opposite side of a neighbour. The consequence of this haphazard arrangement is that at least one petal is covered on both sides by its neighbours. To add a measure of symmetry to this random shaping, it is possible to lever the edge of each petal so that the same edge (either right or left) overlaps its neighbour. If the whole bloom is arranged like this, it can be very pleasing to the eye. It is also very easy to damage the blooms in the process. With edged auriculas, damage is even more likely to ensue, though a few growers have managed the feat successfully. The tradition stipulates roundness and flatness as the great criteria. Some judges dislike the dressing of Edged Auriculas; others think that it can enhance the pips. Attempt it at your peril. A personal view is that, done well, it can be advantageous; done badly, it is an eyesore.

THE TRUSS

A truss approaching the highest standard does not need a human hand to point it out. It will simply stand out for all to see. It is a rare phenomenon, but a delight and a privilege to behold when it occurs. It is comprised of evenly sized pips, all as near to identical as possible. They should just touch each other, but not overlap. The distribution of the pips in the truss should be even. There should be no gaps or conspicuous voids in the head of bloom. It is sad to see a nice head of bloom spoilt by a big space, wide enough for the judges to insert a couple of fingers. The pedicels should be strong enough to hold the pips firmly without sagging and just long enough to prevent any overcrowding within the truss. All immature pips and unopened buds must be removed. They are regarded as imperfections. So too is any trace of padding which has been used between the pips either during growth or to prevent damage during transport. As in so much else in the world of the exhibition auricula, the stipulation is

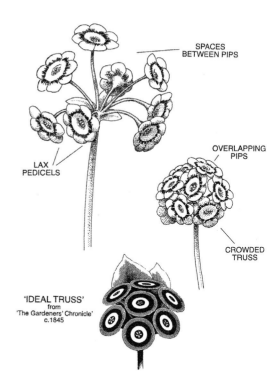

FLOWER TRUSSES

simple but its fulfilment is much more difficult. If your plants don't match up to the criteria for perfection, don't worry overmuch. Try to arrange the individual pips to form a neat head and console yourself with the thought that the majority of exhibitors on show day will experience the same difficulties and doubts.

SELF-COLOURED SHOW AURICULAS

THE PIP IN GENERAL

The standards for the Selfs follow in large measure those traditionally employed for Edged Auriculas. The pips of the Selfs must be round, flat and thrum-eyed. They are usually slightly smaller than the Edges, somewhere around 1⅛in.-1¼in. (29-30mm).

THE TUBE

The tube is usually about one sixth of the pip's diameter but it should be golden, round and topped by fresh anthers, just like those of the edged plants. The problems associated with pale tubes amongst the blue shades are most prominent in the Selfs. The judges know that no one has yet produced a blue with a golden tube but very pale tubes will not meet with approval.

THE PASTE

The paste of many Selfs tends to be narrower than that of the Edges. It should approach about a half of the pip's diameter. If it becomes too narrow, the balance between the coloured outer section and the brilliant white and gold of the inner sections is lost. This is a point to bear in mind if you are tempted to try your hand at breeding new varieties, especially Yellows.

Any angularity of the paste will stand out starkly against the body colour in the Selfs. Five-petalled pips are more prone to this and later pips fail here rather than earlier ones. The judges will keep an eye open too for cracks and marks in the paste of Blue Selfs which seem to be more prone to faulty pastes than plants in the other sections. They should not be staged.

THE BODY

The remainder of the pip is taken up by the coloured section, the body. The groups into which the colours fall are Yellow, Red, Dark, Blue and Any Other Colour. There has been much controversy in the past about the placement of shades such as cream or buff. The consensus arrived at is that only something which is truly yellow belongs in the Yellow class. Paler and darker shades fall under the catch-all, Any Other Colour. Attempts to equate auricula colouring with R.H.S. colour charts have not met with success, the judges lacking time on the day to assess which particular shade matches which card in a swatch and better uses have been found for the finance which would be needed to purchase such an item. The judges' discretion has sufficed until now and one would hope that it might suffice for the future. In cases of controversy, it is easier to change a judge from one year to the next than it is to achieve consensus as to where borders lie at one particular time, only to enter into the difficulties of altering the wording of a specification later when a future generation of growers disagrees.

The main faults with Selfs other than yellow varieties lie in the colouring that gives them their name. This tries to shade out from a darker colour next to the paste to a lighter version at the periphery. When this happens, it is a bad fault, as the plant can hardly then be described as self-coloured. Blues are particularly prone to this failing. Some of the peach or amber shades have a different imperfection which only becomes clear on closer inspection. This is marked veining of darker shades against a lighter background. An even colouring should be the aim. There may also be a tendency for the pips to mature to a slightly different colour from that which they showed when they first emerged. All the pips left on the truss for the judges to view must be of uniform colouring.

PETAL TEXTURE

The final defect of some Selfs, particularly Yellows, is the petal texture. The richness and brilliance of the Selfs relies on solid petals. If they become too thin, they look as if they are ailing and not the opulent beauties which will balance out the more geometrical serenity of their edged cousins.

The general growth and presentation of Selfs is exactly that which we saw earlier for the Edges. Growing Selfs has traditionally been considered to be easier than growing Edges. There has therefore been a bias against them as candidates for Premier medals. Nowadays the judges are more open to the beauty of the Selfs, but beware: the freshness of a Self is more fleeting than that of an Edged variety. It is not unusual to watch them pass their best between staging and the end of a show. This happens most frequently when the plants are allocated a place in direct sunshine without shade. The judges can only assess what stands before them after staging is finished. Plants should be kept out of direct sunlight if possible; the show superintendent may be of assistance to any exhibitor who fears that his or her plants may be put at a disadvantage. A truly excellent Self is another of those rare finds.

MULTI-PLANT CLASSES

The aim of these classes is to display the grower's skill in the cultivation of the plants, to achieve a balance of form and colour in their exhibition and also to show something of the diversity of the forms in the groups of plants stipulated. So what will the judges look for in these classes?

The six-pot class allows the widest choice to the exhibitor. The judges will look for good form and freshness first and will then consider the harmony of the whole. A preponderance of either edged or Self varieties might well take the first prize if they are very fresh and cultivated to the highest standard, but it is unlikely. The judges are not obliged to give a first prize if they consider that the standard of the exhibits is not up to that expected or usually attained. A good selection might comprise four Edges and two Selfs, though three of each category might also find favour. If it is possible to set up one each of a Green Edge, a Grey Edge and a White Edge with a suitable complement, the exhibitor will have the beginnings of a good exhibit. The 4:2 arrangement will permit an edged variety front and rear with two Selfs (and these of different colours) breaking up the Edges and possibly something like a White to contrast with a Green in the centre. A 3:3 group will allow the exhibitor to show three Edges and three Selfs, so opening up the possibility of an edged

variety from each of the three categories and three Selfs of different colours. Supporters of each opinion exchange views on the topic not infrequently. The tradition leans towards the side of the 4:2 camp but well-regarded growers and breeders have recently propounded the case for 3:3. It would be a rare challenge and a huge treat for any judge to be faced with a decision as to which is the better arrangement. Six fine, fresh plants is still the criterion which beats most exhibitors.

In the class for four Show Auriculas, one Self is traditionally considered adequate with as wide a variety of Edges as possible. Multi-plant Self classes should comprise as wide a variety of colours as possible.

If the grower can find the requisite number of good plants to set on the showbench, be that six, four, three or two, the judges will then look at them as a grouped exhibit. They will consider how well matched the plants are. If there is a tight head of pips on one plant and a truss with long, lax pedicels on the other, they can hardly be judged as good companions. It can be like looking at two umbrellas, one with a cloth covering and the other without, showing just its ribs. Finding a whole well-matched group is part of the exhibitor's skill.

The final challenge in the multi-plant classes is matching the height of the stems. The plants have to be shown without any form of artificial aid such as one pot inside another or small blocks to raise the plants. Inevitably, it is very difficult to find a group all of the same height. This has always been a problem but, when it is possible, or when it is engineered by adding or subtracting a little compost at the base of a pot or by re-potting into a different pot, it is a pleasing sight to see. More frequently, a group of plants is presented of slightly different heights which slope down from the tallest at the rear to the shortest at the front. If this is done carefully, with a similar step down from each to its neighbour, it is also an acceptable arrangement. Most judges still consider a group of the same height to be a more difficult attainment.

ALPINE AURICULAS

TYPES

You will be aware by now that the so-called Alpine Auriculas are the brightly-coloured side of the family. They divide into two broad sections. One has a light underlying tissue which approaches white or a very pale cream. The other shows a different range of colours overlying deep yellow tissue. The first group is known as light-centred, the second as gold-centred. The groups result from their wild ancestors which have similar tissues but each possesses a different cell sap acidity. This has an influence on the colouring material which combines with it. There are no Gold Centres with blue colouring and, conversely, no Light Centres with any trace of brown. There are a number of unfortunate varieties in which the tissue is halfway between light and gold. These have never been accepted as true exhibition varieties, even when they approach exhibition form. If you hear a plant described as 'custard-centred', these are the ones concerned. They may be pretty but they will not be reckoned the equal of those with a centre of the prescribed kind.

The main characteristic of the Alpine group is that their blooms are free of farina. It was not uncommon to see this appear on the centre of the plants in the second half of the twentieth century but more recent breeders have all but eliminated it. Any traces of meal stand out strangely against the smooth, bright tissue of a pip and look very much out of place. Farina may appear on the scape but this should not be penalised by the judges. The leaves must never carry any trace of meal, however.

THE TUBE

The characteristics expected of the Alpine Auricula resemble those of the Show types. The tube should be round and smoothly finished. A number of varieties possess a raised rim which was highly regarded by some of the old growers and is still looked upon by some enthusiasts as an advantage, since it emphasises the tube's circularity. Some voices will complain that it stands proud of the flat surface of the corolla and mars its flatness. There is no accepted standard here. If the rim exists, it should serve solely to create a pleasing roundness at the centre of the pip and must not detract from its overall beauty.

The diameter of the tube should be about one sixth of the whole pip, so conforming to the 1:3:6 ratio. It should be either light or golden, matching the colour of the eye, and the anthers should be bright, fresh and even, neatly filling the top of the tube. Varieties with a sparse show of pollen will not be highly regarded by the judges.

The last failing of the tube on some Alpine types is its tendency to be trumpet-shaped or conical at the top. This robs the pip of a neatness and preciseness which can so enhance the brightness of the colours. The standard states that it must be 'well up to the surface of the pip'.

The stigma, as with the Show varieties, should not be visible either above or between the anthers. Pin-eyed plants are always disqualified. The anthers should be of a rich gold or yellow shade, with their pollen as fresh as possible. If the anthers have shed their dust or, worse still, if they carry none, the bloom can look tired or somehow emaciated. In the past odd types were produced which had this fault and were widely grown and shown. Fortunately, present-day breeders have bred better and we shall follow the best traditions if we consign poor anthers to the past.

THE EYE OR CENTRE

The centre of an Alpine Auricula serves to emphasise the brightness of the coloured zone beyond it. It should be light or golden, as already stated, and flow outward from the tube. It must not carry any trace of meal or colouring on the underlying tissue. The centres on many varieties will change slightly in colour as they age, so scrutinise your plant carefully before you put it on the bench.

The outer edge of the centre is also prone to various failings. The first is a bleeding of the colour on the outer section of the petals into the pureness of the eye. It looks almost like ink soaking into soft paper. This spoils the precision of the pip and will not be considered for an award by the judges. A second failing is an angular centre. This was often found in Light Centres, especially in the blue shades. Once again, we have to thank the admirable efforts of the plant breeders who have reduced this fault to such a degree. A further fault, much more difficult to eradicate, is the cutting into the eye by the edges of the petals, as if someone had snipped just a little too far when dividing the petals from each other. Few varieties are entirely free of this. If the petal division continues too far, however, it spoils the circularity and flatness of the centre. The last weakness in the eye which the judges will look for is any sign of corrugation. Like the rest of the pip, the centre must be flat.

The width of the centre should be about, or just over, a half of the pip. If it is too small, the pip can look heavy and lack brightness; if too broad, the eye dominates the whole pip, taking away the effect of the brilliant colours beyond it.

THE BODY

The attraction of the Alpine Auricula lies in the contrast of the eye and the coloured body. This contrast may be bold or more subtle. The colour should start at its darkest where it meets the central eye and shade out gradually to a lighter version of the same colour at the periphery. This leads to the vinous shades of red suffusing out to almost pink and a deep night-time blue to a light and airy lavender blue in the Light Centres, while the Gold Centres show a depth of colour verging on black adjacent to the eye which flows out to brilliant red, flame or brown at the rim. The change in colour has to be gentle and gradual. Laced Alpines have their enthusiasts and even the odd class at the shows, but too abrupt a change from dark to light will not find favour with the judges in the general classes.

The outer part of the flower also needs to be flat and round with evenly sized petals which carry no notch. Any pips which show any sign of corrugation round the eye or which display pips carrying petals with any hint of curling at the edge should be removed. On some pips individual petals cockle (curl upwards.) On others the whole pip is cup-shaped. On yet others the petals bend backwards, known as reflexing. All are faults and will be penalised by the judges. Only flat blooms are appropriate.

The whole pip should be about the same size as a Self Show Auricula, namely about 1⅛in. (29mm). Some varieties have a natural vigour which leads to their producing very large pips. They must not be allowed to become coarse. Good Alpines should look pert, neat and bright.

The lay of the petals sometimes leads to a controversy as to their best organisation. Just as the exhibitors of Show and Self varieties flatten their plants, if they are not by nature sufficiently flat, so some exhibitors of Alpine varieties like to lift the edge of some petals so that each one overlaps its neighbour on the same side all the way round the bloom. This is known as dressing. When done well, there can be little doubt that it can enhance the natural beauty of the pip. When done badly, it can damage the petals. Occasionally a plant may produce a pip shaped like this of its own accord, but it is rare. The judges are looking for freshness, roundness, neatness and brightness. If the plant does not possess these qualities by nature, no amount of dressing will induce them. Should two plants be evenly matched in these qualities, the judges may prefer the geometrical precision of the dressed plant, though nothing in the tradition states that this must be so.

THE TRUSS AND SCAPE

Alpine Auriculas tend to be more vigorous and less genetically complex than the Show types. It is therefore more common to find good examples at the shows. It is also easier to be content with less than prime presentation of a good specimen. The judges will look for the same features as in the Show section. The truss should be neat and compact without being crowded. The pips should just adjoin each other and be borne on strong pedicels. All the pips should be of the same colour, not always easy with some varieties which change as they mature. The lay of the truss should be even with no gaps or lolling pips. All immature or unopened buds must be removed, for anything which is not a perfect bloom is counted as a fault. Any traces of padding used during training and transport must also be cleared out.

The scape should be firm and again between 4in. and 7in. (10cm and 18cm) in length. It may be staked neatly, either to aid its positioning or to prevent damage on the way to the show, but the tie which secures the stem to the stake should not interfere with the footstalks or it may be construed as an illicit aid.

GENERAL PRESENTATION AND MULTI-PLANT CLASSES

The remarks made concerning the Show varieties apply also to plants in the Alpine classes. The foliage should be neat and provide a reasonable covering on the top of the pot. Where feasible, colours should be selected to display the range possible inside the groups. The perfect group would comprise equal representations of centres and body colours, with trusses nicely matched for number and size of pips and with a similar formation of the truss. Above all, the judges look for a group of fresh, bright flowers.

DOUBLE AURICULAS

Double Auriculas came to prominence only in the second half of the twentieth century. There is, therefore, no tradition of desirable properties or of weaknesses in them. Standards which have emerged have resulted from the thinking of those who bred them, those who admired them and those who were required to judge them. In this group the breeders and their efforts must take the greatest praise, for they have raised what was once a group of ragamuffins to be enjoyed out in the rough and tumble of the garden border to a level of beauty, of form and grace which would often be the equal of jewellery or plasterwork fit to grace any stately home and its collections. The path to the present standards is not without its controversies and others will doubtless ensue, but what follows are the thoughts which have held sway amongst the judges in recent years.

GENERAL PRESENTATION

The presentation of Double Auriculas is exactly the same as already described for Show and Alpine types. The judges will look for neat, fresh plants, well arranged to show the diversity now available. Individual examples should be of the same height as the other classifications and a stand of plants in the multi-plant classes should be even and neat. Foliage may be green or mealed but always fresh and clean.

THE PIP

No set format exists for the lay of the petals in Double Auriculas. Originally their Border Auricula origins brought frilly and notched pips but few of these appear nowadays. Most varieties seen on the showbench display a smooth edge to the individual petals. This contributes to the demand made of exhibition auriculas that they should be round in outline. It is unlikely that anything less than a circular pip will be accepted for the foreseeable future.

The number of petal layers has also varied as the plants have been developed. The prime demand has always been that the tube should be hidden. Initially this led to varieties with little more than a layer of outer petals and then a raised inner set which covered the tube, the whole arrangement resembling the blooms of a crested French marigold. The breeders have moved further and further away from this type and the plants seen on the bench lean increasingly towards the shape of the old roses or the newer English Roses with their quartered and buttoned blooms. The main feature the judges seek is neatness and roundness of outline.

The colours to be found in Double Auriculas are open to constant development. The brightness of Alpine Auriculas has so far not been reached but many attractive shades have graced the benches. The question of shading of colour in the individual pip, as happens in the Alpine Auriculas, also plays no role in the judges' deliberations. The only stipulation is that the colouring of all the pips in the truss should be the same. This means that if the grower has a plant on which the outer petals are a darker shade than the inner ones, then the gradation of colouring should be the same on all the pips left in the truss.

Meal may also be present either as paste or stripes. It should not, however, smear untidily across the coloured tissue and it should be consistent throughout the truss. Given the usual connection between stripes and unevenness of the rim of the pip, the grower should look to circularity of the pip as the first consideration, before all thoughts of novelty, as this will be the judges' prime consideration.

THE TRUSS AND SCAPE

The trusses on some Double Auriculas are quite sizeable and it is not unknown for the scape to come too short to hold it clear of the leaves. The judges will look for the same length of stem as in the other auricula classes, namely 4in.-7in. (10cm-18cm). The other fault which mars the appearance of some otherwise well-shaped trusses lies in their footstalks. Early examples of Doubles often had weak pedicels which caused the pips to droop. This has been largely eliminated by the breeders and it would not please any judge now. There is also a problem which arises when the footstalks are sturdy but short. This leaves the pips lying too close together, causing them to press against their neighbours and lose their circular outline. Judicious culling early in their growth or shortly before the show might be beneficial. The judges are looking for a handsome exhibition plant, not a nosegay.

STRIPED AURICULAS

The Stripes were a 1970s introduction to the showbench but they have seen a major increase in the types of bloom, the quality and size of pips and the quality of striping in as short a time as the period since the mid-1990s. Since their blooms are composed of two different kinds of tissue which both run out from the central paste towards the periphery of the pips, it should come as no surprise to discover that the tissue types grow at different rates. This leads to an unevenness in the rim of the individual blooms. The only (and rare) exception is when the periphery carries a China edge of meal, leaving a single line of mealy tissue running round the pips. In the few varieties where this happens, the pips may more nearly approach the ideal of a circular shape. Some growers of a conservative bent regard anything which deviates from the classical form as anathema. Others see the re-introduction of the striped plant as a widening of the gene pool and a re-acceptance of what the very earliest florists would have treasured. The result is that judging Stripes has been very much down to the interpretation of individuals. Recently the Midlands and West Section of the N.A.P.S. has codified its views into a cohesive form. These are a reliable base from which to judge these plants.

THE PIP

As in the standard classes, only thrum-eyed plants are admissible. The anthers should be fresh and bold, while the tube should not exceed one-sixth of the pip's diameter. The paste should be just the same as is found in the Edged and Self Show Auriculas, namely solid, white, fine and smooth. It should stretch to a half of the pip's diameter. The judges appreciate that the individual bloom may not be perfectly circular but it should be as round as possible. The nibbled edge to the pips should not detract from the overall attractiveness. The individual pip should be about 1⅛in. (29mm) across. The petals should be evenly striped with lines running the full width of the area between the paste and the petal edge. It is important that neither the stripes nor the colour between them should clump together to form anything which resembles either the ring of the ground in the Edged varieties nor a block of edge tissue. If any plants look at all like a failed Edged Auricula, the judges may not be too kindly disposed towards them.

THE TRUSS AND SCAPE

A little care and attention to detail will pay off just as much with this type of plant as with the others. As the plants are growing, care must be taken to support the stems with a stake. With some of the older varieties the scapes are not as robust as one might hope and, if the blooms should bow their heads on a warm day, the striping may smear. Few of the Stripes throw tightly clustered trusses but, with the few that do, they should be separated with a little cotton wool to give them room. The exhibitor must, however, make certain that none of this is left when the plant goes on to the bench. The scape itself should be the requisite 4in.-7in. (10cm-18cm) in height.

GENERAL PRESENTATION

The plants should be kept as fresh as possible before they are exhibited. Fresh, unblemished foliage over the top of the pot sets off the blooms nicely. If the grower is fortunate enough to encounter a class for more than one plant, try to present varieties which either harmonise in form and colour or which demonstrate the possibilities of the Stripes. The current maximum number in multi-pot classes for Stripes is two. In such a case, two plants of equal height with the same number of pips are ideal, but if one is slightly taller than the other, set the taller one at the back.

Stripes on showbench.

Chapter 8
Pests, Diseases and How to Deal With Them

Despite the list of troubles which follows, the auricula is not one of the more difficult plants to cultivate. The pests with a taste for it are not hugely different from many others round the garden.

Aphids of all colours may affect your plants. Those on the foliage are easily dealt with by remedies both organic and inorganic or even by the florist's finger and thumb. A more troublesome kind may attack the plants' roots. It is covered in a white fluff which, while being quite distinctive, helps to defend it against contact insecticide. You may spot an infestation by the appearance of a white furry collar round the neck of your plants or by a sickly appearance to the leaves and general growth. If the pest is indeed present, you will see it on roots round the edge of the rootball. It is possible to touch individuals lightly with a small paintbrush dipped in methylated spirits but care must be taken to keep the liquid clear of the root surface. Any systemic insecticide will see off this problem. It also obviates any regular need to remove the plant from its pot.

Caterpillars, slugs and snails can cause a lot of damage if you do not spot them in time. Even a small beast of this kind can consume a considerable amount of food. There is one small, green caterpillar which is difficult to spot against green foliage and which homes in on the heart of the leaf cone with its fresh growth. Look for any sort of holes in or round the leaves. Removal by hand is the simplest remedy when you encounter these nuisances.

Vine weevil continues to constitute one of the more serious threats to Auriculas. Fortunately, with the insecticides and predators now available to the amateur grower, they can be beaten. Constant vigilance is needed,

however. Adult weevils are brown-black beetles about ⅜in. (1cm) in length with a black snout. They cannot fly. They nibble semi-circular holes in the edge of the foliage and lay their eggs in the surface of the compost. These hatch out into white grubs, about ⅜in. (1cm) long, with a small brown head. They curl up into a question mark and nourish themselves at a frightening rate on the fresh, white roots of your plants. If the leaves on any pot begin to look at all limp and unhealthy, waggle the top of the plant a little. If it feels loose in the compost, it is worth tapping out the rootball to check its condition. Should you find even one white grub, shake off all the compost and dispose of it. Then re-pot using fresh compost and a clean pot before placing the affected plant in a cool spot to recover. Most plants will send out fresh root growth but less vigorous ones can suffer badly. Chemical control is possible through sprays based on thiacloprid, a development of the earlier imidacloprid. Bottles of this pesticide are available from High Street shops and garden centres. Predatory nematodes *(Steinernema kraussei,* tiny parasitic eel worms) provide an organic solution to the problem but they require care in application and may die out if they have no more food to hand or if the soil temperature falls below 41°F (5°C).

The organic grower might also be interested in one other possible (though not easy) natural remedy. Over the course of fifteen years with a greenhouse in a wet garden on the hills of northern England. I remained unaffected by vine weevil. The only reason I could ever come up with was that throughout most of the year a channel of water persisted round the outside of the greenhouse, my 'moat' as it became known. Vine weevils cannot fly and they certainly cannot swim. It has been reported that some old florists put the legs of their staging into containers of water as a protection against pests. Although a bucket might be a little cumbersome in this position, something like a small, plastic ice cream container might not be too objectionable.

Red spider mite is a pest which has appreciated the hot, dry air of recent summers. A cool, moist atmosphere around your plants will help to deter the mites from taking up residence in the first place. Providing your Auriculas with a cool and shady home for the summer helps to keep this pest at bay. If they should attack your plants, you may be sure that they will go first for those with mealy leaves. Meal-free varieties are definitely second on the menu. A close examination of the leaves will reveal a paler, mottled look, even between individual grains of farina. The foliage will then turn a greyish white; it has had much of the goodness sucked out of it. A severe attack will also lead to tiny webs being formed by the mites between adjacent surfaces of the plants. The mites themselves are tiny and usually prefer the underside of the leaves, though when the population starts to spread they will also occupy the upper part. They are just visible to the naked eye but more readily seen with a magnifying glass.

Chemical remedies exist but you must read the instructions on the packaging carefully. Few of the sprays or drenches on the market are totally effective. The experience of most growers is that a spray containing an emulsion of some sort will kill many of the pests, though a further application may be needed to get rid of any beasts which hatch out after the spray has been applied. Mites in one greenhouse or frame may also not react in the same way as others not far away and resistance to some pesticides is widespread.

Again, a biological control is available. *Phytoseiulus persimilis* is a mite with an appetite for red spider mite. It demands certain conditions, such as a minimum temperature of 50°F (10°C), but it reproduces more quickly than the red spider and will eat all stages of the pest. It needs to be applied in good time, however, and a cold spell immediately after application can hinder its development and effectiveness or even wipe it out, thus necessitating a second (not inexpensive) purchase.

White fly bears a strong resemblance to a tiny white moth but it breeds rapidly and sucks the sap from plants. Chemical sprays will kill some of them but *Encarsia,* a tiny black and yellow parasitic wasp about ⅒in. (1mm) in length is more efficient, though it too needs a specified temperature to carry out its good work. Despite the prevalence of white fly in many British greenhouses, there are no reports of serious attacks on auriculas, though the grower should always be aware that the pest may suddenly develop a taste for the primula tribe.

Grey mould (*Botrytis cinerea*) attacks many garden plants. It thrives in cool, moist conditions and takes great delight in setting up home on tardy, watery leaves in late autumn. There are sprays to deal with it, but the simplest course of action is to remove at least that part of the leaf which is suffering or to take away the whole leaf. The latter, though more drastic, is the way that things will probably develop in any case, as most leaves with any grey mould will usually die right down to the main stem, but, if the poor plant in question is not blessed with an abundance of foliage, leaving it with even a small piece of greenery may help it to gather some reserves of strength.

Rot may attack either the roots or the carrot. A few roots will die back in the course of the year and may be removed at any time, especially when re-potting, but a general decay of the roots should lead you to consider either your compost or your growing regime. There is probably too much water round the root system for it to thrive. Re-settling a plant with a modicum of root rot into fresh, more open compost may help it to survive. Trim away all dead roots before re-potting.

Rot at the base of the carrot is not an uncommon occurrence. You will often find it when re-potting. Scrape or cut away all brown tissue until you see a nice, white surface right across the base of the carrot. Treat this with a dusting of fungicide or flowers of sulphur and re-pot as usual. If you have even a few healthy roots to sustain the plant, it should pick up again. Rot round the collar of the plant is a more serious matter. Any brown or grey band in this area should be treated as suspicious, especially if the central cone of undeveloped leaves starts to lean to one side. If you gently scrape or cut away at the band of discoloration, you will soon find whether it is a surface blemish or a rot infection. In the former case, dust with a fungicide or flowers of sulphur and leave the wound to dry out. If you are unfortunate and the rot has penetrated further into the main stem, work into it gently with a sharp implement such as a good knife or your finger nail, remove the rot and treat the affected area as above. If it has not gone too far into the stem, the plant may survive, though it is likely to be weakened for a season. If the rot has penetrated beyond the centre of the main stem, look for any buds which may be breaking below that point. If there should be a few, chop off the growth on the main stem just below the rot and treat the remaining stump with a fungicide. The buds should develop into new offsets to continue the stock. Even if no buds are visible, it is worthwhile removing the crown at a point just beneath the rot, putting the pot to one side and waiting to see whether new buds develop from below the surface of the compost. It may mean waiting right through the winter for the new green shreds of hope, but it does happen. Should there be any sign of new root growth above the rot, re-pot the top of the plant (with all rot removed) into fresh compost, keep it cool and hope.

Good hygiene is the best way of maintaining a healthy stock. Compost should be as fresh as possible and pots should be clean. A regular programme of pot-washing is essential unless the grower has access to unlimited supplies of new pots. A little washing-up liquid in the water usually suffices to remove most dirt, though an overnight soaking may be needed to soften any encrustations or hard deposits, especially on clay pots. After that, a good washing-up brush or a scouring pad will see off most dirt. For ultimate cleansing, you may wish to put a very small amount of disinfectant or even domestic bleach into the washing water, but do wear gloves when you scrub the pots and do omit these cleaning fluids if you are in any doubt as to the quantity needed. It is not only neat but also good practice either to clean or to replace plant labels so that they do not carry over diseases or pests from an old pot to a new one. Washing dirty pots and labels in winter or early spring is not the most attractive employment but it is essential in good cultivation.

If you use a knife to trim either the carrot or roots, it is advisable to keep a pot of a sterilising solution to hand where you can clean the knife blade after you have finished applying it to any plant. This should prevent the spread of viruses or other diseases from one plant to the next. The solution is usually either methylated spirits or a bleach of some kind. It may sound like adding extra layers of work to what is supposed to be a relaxing hobby, but it soon becomes just a tiny extra which occupies only a few seconds and which leaves the florist with full confidence that he or she has done all that is possible to keep the treasures in good health.

Chapter 9
AND NOW?

In the first chapter of this book I tried to set out the many changes which have befallen the auricula in the course of the last five hundred or so years. It has evolved from two small Alpine plants, each with its own individual colour, through the x *pubescens* hybrids with their much wider range of colour and habit, the acquisition of stripes, the increase in the number of its petals to build up the double forms and the acquisition of leaf tissue in the blooms, all giving us the range that we know today. It has been a favourite of simple country-dwellers, landed gentry, clerics and scholars, skilled artisans and now of the widest spectrum of enthusiasts. It has been appreciated for its herbal properties, its bright colours, its scent and its ability to provide blooms which equate to the formality of a rose window, a sonnet or a string quartet. After a period in the doldrums for much of the twentieth century, the auricula is now showing something of a resurgence. How then might it develop and what might be the challenges which confront the Florists of the future?

The prime concern must be the climate. The auricula developed originally in the Alps where the plants are never subject to constantly high temperatures. In the winter, the plants lie dormant but are insulated from the worst of the cold by a thick covering of snow. Growers across the world know how problematical auriculas can be, if they do not experience a decent winter rest. Even in the milder areas of the U.K. a warm winter means early blooms on gangling stems with small, pale pips of diminished beauty. If our climate continues to change and raise temperatures across the planet, parts of Western Europe, the U.S.A., Canada and Tasmania may no longer be able to offer appropriate conditions for the plants to prosper. Little can be done to offer immediate alleviation to the pains of the current generations of Florists. One can but hope that new growers will emerge in latitudes which are cooler and that both plants and enthusiasm are passed on.

Composts have always been a subject of much debate and sometimes of myth, magic and obfuscation. The general tenet of providing an open mixture of clean soil, additional humus and some drainage material continues unchanged. The sourcing of good soil and humus is another matter. Considerable doubts have been expressed as to the quality of much of the soil sold by commercial outlets in the U.K. It has been known to vary from the sandy to mixtures containing large amounts of clay. Weeds still germinate in auricula pots, despite the supposed sterilisation of the soil prior to its being bagged for sale. The growers of previous generations recommended soil from below the grassy layer of an established meadow provided that it was not too heavy. They were also keen on the fine soil thrown up in molehills. Not everyone has access to an established meadow, though some will have the dubious privilege of molehills round their garden. Should a mole have taken a liking to your patch, it may be worthwhile just running the contents of one of its little hills through your fingers. The animal's claws break up the soil into the finest particles. It may not be sterilised but it may form the foundation for a good compost, provided that drainage material such as Perlite or grit and a good measure of humus can be added to prevent it from coagulating into an impenetrable block in the pot.

An alternative source of soil may lie in one of the other fashionable pursuits of this first decade of the twentieth century and that is the vegetable garden. Many more gardeners are producing their own food. Any patch of ground used for growing vegetables will be subject to regular cultivation and will have been broken to some extent by the roots of the crops thrusting through it. Soil improved in this way may form the basis of composts, should our present sources no longer be available.

Given that a grower has access to a reliable supply of soil, what then remains to be done? The answer here is not totally black and white. The soil used for the cultivation of any plant in a pot should be sterilised, if we wish to be certain that pests and disease organisms do not have immediate access to it. The process of sterilisation is not an easy one for the home grower. Devices are available to achieve this end. They are metal boxes into which the soil is loaded and a constant temperature of approximately 85 degrees is applied for about ninety minutes. This is an optimal regime but the purchase price of over £300 (2009 price) for a small model with a capacity of about thirty-four litres will deter nearly every individual amateur. A small co-operative, on the other hand, might consider acquiring one. Scalding soil with boiling water has been used but the natural crumb structure is totally destroyed and this is not to be recommended. Domestic microwave ovens are also employed by some but again the grower must take care not to destroy the soil structure in the process. The smell which arises from any body of heated soil will also preclude the use of any kitchen equipment, if the grower shares a house with non-enthusiasts and wishes to continue to do so. If it is not feasible to hold the requisite temperature for an hour and a half, the grower may be faced with the possibility of using unsterilized soil in his growing medium. This was the practice of older generations and has been used by the author whose garden lies on the red-brown, fertile marl of Worcestershire. The soil was put into a box for several months and allowed to dry out thoroughly. It was then crumbled finely and mixed with a commercial soilless compost and grit in the recommended 4:2:2 ratio. No difference could be seen between plants grown in the home-made mix and those in commercial composts. Should you decide to follow this route, you must be aware that natural organisms may still be present which might damage your plants. You must also ensure good drainage, if your soil is at all heavy, and enough humus, should your garden soil be sandy or gritty. Above all, be prepared to weed your pots throughout the growing season.

Good humus is a much more contentious matter. The most popular form for many years was peat. With the determination to remove peat from the horticultural scene came the challenge to seek out an alternative which provided the same capability to open up soil and yet also to hold water without becoming saturated. So far, no single product has shown itself to be the equal of peat, though many are approaching that stage. Coir, a fibrous by-product of coconut production, is widely used, though questions have been raised as to the efficacy of transporting it round the world. It has been argued that the use of fossil fuels to do so is not in keeping with our desire to slow down climate change. Some Florists have also complained that it does not retain water in the growing medium to the same degree as peat. A recent innovation has been the use of fine, soft fibres of wood added to other material such as peat. This is proving quite successful. One can but hope that similar improvements will continue.

But what can be found in the environment of most home gardeners which will aid our

An Auricula theatre. This formed a part of the display put on by the Midland and West Section of the National Auricula and Primula Society at the Malvern Spring Show in 2008. To the right is a *Primula sieboldii*, shown in a traditional Japanese pot. *P. sieboldii* is cultivated for display in Japan in the same way as the auricula elsewhere in the world.

desire to recycle material around us and still encourage the most beautiful plants? The growers of old used manure and leaf mould. Horse or cow manure was rotted for at least two years and used either in the compost or, better still, as a top dressing in spring. Adding manure to a growing medium is fraught with problems. Should it retain any of its freshness, the roots of the auricula may be burned and rot. A top dressing allows the food in the manure to be washed through gradually. Again, it must be free of any unpleasant odours, if the grower is to be at all sure that it will not damage his or her plants. Only once was I fortunate enough to be given a quantity of old cow manure which had lain forgotten in a farmer's shed for several years. When applied as a thin layer on the top of the pots in early spring and developed into a spongy layer much like a garden mulch, the plants grew vigorously and threw beautiful blooms.

Given that few will have access to such luxurious additions as old cow manure, what else might be to hand? Many gardeners have

'Joel', a Show Self seen by some as blue and by others as purple

'Watchet'. A pale blue Self mentioned with Blue Steel and Derwentwater as a break from the traditional lines. This points one way towards possible future lines.

access to trees. Leaf mould was the other addition to a good compost which the Florists of earlier generations employed. Most deciduous trees provide a valuable amount, though oak leaves are to be avoided, as they may take much longer to rot down and also produce small amounts of substances which could damage the plants. Evergreens are also to be avoided. Stacking any other leaves in a sheltered spot where the wind cannot blow them away or storing them in bags with holes punched into the bottom and sides is the usual way of making leaf mould. Unfortunately, the process is a lengthy one and may demand two or three years to complete. It is, however, a way for us to help ourselves to grow fine plants and to reduce our demands on the environment.

Housing the auricula poses less of a challenge. Greenhouses and frames are still available at very reasonable prices. The writer

'Night Eyes', a new Dark Self with just a suggestion of purple in its sheen. Another hint of something new for the future.

still uses a small model acquired second-hand via a local newspaper for £50. Even at the time of purchase it carried the patina of age which aluminium assumes and it has continued to give fine service for ten years since then. With both wooden and metal models readily available, it is unlikely that accommodation for the plants will prove a problem. The auricula theatre mentioned in Chapter 1 is also showing signs of revival (see page 149). Although it is possible to purchase beautiful examples as either free-standing structures or in a form to attach to a wall, many have opted to attach stout shelves to outside walls and provide them with a small roof and sides to protect the plants from the worst of the weather. If you should decide to grow plants in this way, make sure that they have adequate light. Shade is needed in the brightest days of the warm seasons but gloom will cause plants to stretch for light. Insects have ready access to

blooms which are totally open like this. Alpine, Double or Border auriculas will not show a bee's footprints but Show, Striped or Fancy varieties which carry either paste or a mealy edge are easily damaged. Plants should be purchased with this caveat in mind.

And what of the plants themselves? The first concern is that the growers must continue to come up with new breeding. The Florists of the early nineteenth century had Edged and Self varieties carrying a variety of body colours. The concentration on black seemed to preclude other grounds, despite the concomitant rise of the brightly coloured Alpines. This led to the point where these other grounds in Show types were derided and the types which proved difficult to categorise were dismissed. Fortunately, this attitude has changed and breeders are actively seeking to re-introduce forms which would have been known to those earlier growers

New Orange Self Show, a seedling from Brian Coop

Green Edge with yellow ground. Condemned in the past as a Fancy but now accepted into the mainstream of Edged types. This one has a neat body colour, a feature which is rare in yellow grounds.

and have fallen out of favour. Green Edges with a bright red body or Grey Edges with a bright red or blue ground could be a delight for the eye. Green paired with a solid brown might also attract the attention of the innocent eye. The problem as ever is that the

A class for six Alpines. This is the largest class at the national shows and contains a mixture of both Light and Gold Centres.

auricula is reticent to couple the colouring with the good proportions which make the difference between a refined bloom and a garish blob.

The Selfs have traditionally retained their groupings of Yellow, Red, Dark and Blue with the catch-all 'Any Other Colour.' The latter was once a small niche for oddities which did not quite conform but is now the focus of considerable attention. The efforts of Brian and Tim Coop were mentioned in the list of varieties. A few other courageous souls have ventured into the same area but it is chiefly to the Coops, *père et fils,* that we owe the present Selfs in light blue, pink, lavender and brown. Other colours are in the pipeline. In 2009 Brian Coop showed an Orange Self with a bright colour and shining paste. Here is a further pointer to the future. There must be others who share this vision and enthusiasm

Gold Centre Alpine 'Hearts of Gold'

to widen the pool of colour (see page 152).

The traditional categories of Edged Auricula retain their reticence to permit the easy production of new plants. Since the retirement of David Hadfield from the auricula-breeding scene, the flow of new edged plants has been much diminished. Complaints have been heard that it seems much harder to produce seed from standard varieties than it was a few years ago. There is no way that we can be dogmatic as to what is

happening. It may be that the plants we are using to provide both seed and pollen are ageing and becoming less fertile. It may be that by using exclusively the Hadfield plants we are going round in circles and simply re-breeding examples of his line. Certainly, the author has put a seedling from 'Figaro' alongside the parent and found it difficult to distinguish between the two. It may also be that we are not as adept as David Hadfield at spotting two potentially good parents and

Alpine seedling of the Laced type – a possible line of development for the future.

persuading them to throw adequate seed. Bob Taylor and Brian Coop have used either more difficult Hadfield plants such as 'Jupiter' or even varieties completely outside the line such as 'Orb' and 'Hew Dalrymple'. 'Roberto' was one parent of Ken Whorton's beautiful 'Prosperine.' Here may be signposts to the future. Anyone who follows this path must be aware that it will not an easy one. Good Green Edges never were plentiful and it is unlikely that they ever will be. The author has

taken a slightly different tack which has thus far not given good results but which has improved with time. Some of the older Fancy varieties such as 'Hinton Fields' have perfectly good centres and paste. Their faults lie with the vast expanse of yellow ground. Crossing them with standard types has led to a plethora of equally unsuitable yellow grounds but every now and then the odd example of red, brown or even black body. A 2006 cross threw three plants with a bright green edge, black

'Fantasia' – very scarce, capricious and not at all vigorous but the type of rarity favoured by the Florists of the 17th and 18th centuries

Striped Double Auricula 'Lincoln Halo'

'Scrumpy', another New Stripe

'Henry's Bane', a striking striped variety

body and good paste. The tube, however, was pale, though smooth and round. After ten years of work, many would say that this line of enquiry has little to commend it. The author hopes to persist nonetheless.

Grey Edged are equally problematical. Many modern varieties owe their parentage to 'Teem,' a fine plant but often marred by a crenated tube. Its offspring have a tendency to carry the same fault. 'Grey Hawk' no longer has its original form and vigour but may offer a means of breeding smoother tubes, while some of the Ward plants such as 'Brookfield' also show the same property. Again, a look at a plant such as 'Hawkwood' will reveal a smooth-rimmed tube with a bright, clean paste. As one of the parents of 'Grey Hawk' it may have other benefits to offer as a parent. Be aware though that it may also pass on its propensity to throw cupped pips and an over-wide ground. A Grey with a clean body and a smoothly rimmed tube

Border Auricula 'Silas'.

Border Auricula 'Dales Red' illustrates the type of more brightly coloured Border Auricula now coming from some of the breeders.

Border Auricula shown by Pat and Robin Fisher, 'Old-Fashioned'

remains one of the challenges to the breeder.

Alpines have come in waves of colour as breeders come up with new forms. As was noted earlier, the red of 'Blossom' was the dominant colour of the 1970s until the advent of the new brown shades of 'Finchfield' and 'Andrea Julie.' These gained companions in the less brilliant browns of 'Sirius' and its offspring. 'Blyth Spirit' and 'Vera' are now adding something to the redder side of the spectrum while the orange-browns continue to increase in both number and brilliance. A similar line of development may be seen in the Light Centres where deep carmines, light pinks and bright blues stage comebacks. In this sphere we can only retain our faith in the skill and insight of the breeders who do constantly come up with good new plants.

Border Auricula 'Bellamy Pride'

Opposite: European hybrids for the garden border

Two types of Alpine passed out of favour but each has its own supporters. The unshaded Alpine is a contradiction in terms to some and a potential beauty to others. So far no modern breeder has come up with an example of this type. A second group is now being looked upon a little more favourably, namely the Laced Alpine. The tradition demands a gentle shading out from dark to light in the body colour but the odd examples of plants where the transition is sudden have pleased the eye of a number of growers. It behoves us to look carefully at these plants and see whether they merit a place amongst the traditional types.

The future of the Doubles is much debated amongst the section's adherents. The degree of doubling has improved to the point where the Florist's demand for a covered centre is catered for in all types now coming from the breeders.

Fancy Auricula 'Little Amber'

The number of petals per pip has ranged in the past from the scant to the over-generous. The aim has to be for the pips to remain double but neat. This has been largely achieved and the debate now centres on the lay of the petals. The question is whether blooms should be imbricated (overlapped like the tiles on a Roman roof) or scrolled like the centres of an old rose. It has been suggested that we return to an earlier grouping of formal and informal types. Such a division would seem to many to be a backward step and an unnecessary move, provided that we can ensure that both forms enjoy equal status in the eyes of all, but the debate remains and future developments may require the supporters of the Double auricula to sit down and discuss those properties of the blooms which attract them in order to formulate guidelines for show days.

Two new forms have begun to emerge which will cause the supporters of the Doubles to ponder. One is the new breed of Striped Double primarily from Derek Salt. Voices have been heard to maintain that they do not belong with plants of a uniform colour. This then raises the question as to whether a plant whose pips carry different colours or different shades of the same colour can be considered as uniform. But what if all pips show the same variation? Does that constitute uniformity? A comparable question must arise as the shading in the colours of the Alpine begins to emerge in the Doubles. This is a line of breeding already being pursued and likely to continue. If the plants exist, we need to ponder what it is about them which pleases our eye.

The Stripes are the most recent section to be added to the auricula clan. After a subdued beginning they are becoming ever more popular and never fail to evoke expressions of admiration from casual visitors to spring shows. It seems likely that they will maintain their place in the auricula world and add new colours to the range which already exists. This is a group of plants which deserves a greater number of breeders. Anyone seeking to provide beautiful plants to the ranks of the auricula might well look at this section.

Border auriculas seem to be attracting the attention of an ever greater number of gardeners and enthusiasts. Old names such as 'Dusty Miller' are still seen on sale and are a decorative addition to many an April garden, but new names are arriving each year. Their ability to put up stout stems and weather-proof blooms is the prime concern of the breeders and a pleasing number are achieving this. The tradition has long been that this type should be of a quieter disposition than the flamboyant exhibition varieties which are kept under the cover of the frame or greenhouse but that is beginning to change. A few varieties of bolder colouring and more extrovert personality such

A group of Fancy Auriculas.

as 'Dales Red' (see page 158) are appearing in the nurserymen's lists. Whether those who prefer the Borders to other categories of auricula will continue to accept the brighter forms into the ranks remains to be seen but one has a suspicion that the members of the general public on the look-out for auriculas to enliven their garden borders might be drawn to the new types.

The last group of auriculas is the most neglected and potentially quite contentious. Its members are those plants which refuse to conform to any established category and are condemned to be known as Fancies. With all Florists' flowers, oddities will insist on cropping up from perfectly conventional varieties. All modern types of pansy, for example, came from a group originally known as Fancy Pansies. Sweet Peas have been bred from the Spencer line which was an aberrant variation on the older, smaller and unruffled types which had gone before. Unfortunately, the Fancy group of auriculas has been used as both a home for new breaks – the Stripes, for example, were originally exhibited as Fancies when there were so few of them that it was impossible to establish a new category – and also, less beneficially, for any plant which might be unusual or colourful but lacked either form, proportion or refinement. Examples of the latter are the older green-edged, yellow-bodied types such as 'Spring Meadows' and 'Hinton Fields.' A look back at the list of varieties in Chapter 4 will reveal that 'Crimple' is just such a plant but of more recent provenance. For years, such plants were left to the personal tastes of any individual who took pleasure in their springtime brightness but they were left out of consideration by the purists whose prime interest was plants of classical formation.

Since the 1990s it has become possible to stage any plants of a non-black ground amongst all the traditional types on the regular showbench provided that they conform to the conventions of form and proportion. Thus it has been known for edged plants with a purple or blue body to be found amongst the prizewinners at national shows. They are certainly very popular amongst those who grow auriculas for their own pleasure without any intention of exhibiting. But the Fancies section has now been broadened by the introduction of plants which can only be described as shaded Selfs. To the traditionalist this is an oxymoron. Looked at objectively, those seen in public so far have a round tube, a solid, white circular paste and a round periphery. The best example is probably Henry Pugh's 'Little Amber,' (see page 162) a plant whose name derives from that of his grand-daughter but which neatly describes the blooms, for they shade out from a light orange nearest to the paste to a slightly tinted shade of cream at the very rim. Were others to follow with the same circularity and proportions, the question would have to be asked whether this constituted a new group or was merely an odd deviation from the accepted norm. Some exhibitors have been heard to ask how on show day a distinction may be drawn between the edged type of Fancy and the shaded Self form. The author offers no easy solution to the question. It is to be hoped that the growers will approach this and similar questions with an open mind and a degree of common sense. If the plants remain rare or fail to attract any popularity, no categorisation needs to be made. Should the opposite be the case, it would seem reasonable for those with an interest in them to sit down and think what it is in this form that appeals to the human eye and to put it into words. There should be no rush to precipitate acceptance but likewise no reticence to be open to new lines of thought.

The availability of plants to the general public is an area of some optimism. Every spring more seem to be on sale both by specialists and by general nurseries and garden centres. Micro-propagation has helped to bring auriculas to more people. It may have

'Northern Blue'. A darker sister to the light blue of 'Denim' and one of the additions to the shaded Selfs.

the weaknesses that were commented on earlier (variability of plants and susceptibility to old viruses) but one hopes that the botanists who carry out the process will become increasingly adept with their little plants. If they fail to do so, they will be storing up disappointment and disenchantment for which no Florist would wish.

Even after over thirty years growing auriculas, I am still all too aware of the surprises which befall me each season. I am also aware of the great goodwill and generosity of my fellow growers. My main hope is that an open mind and the same magnanimous spirit will continue in the future to bring an appreciation of the auricula's serene beauty to those who each year find the flowers for that first, exciting time.

Envoi

Since this book first appeared in 2009, the number of growers producing new and exciting plants has shown a remarkable increase. Fresh possibilities are being explored and splendid new varieties are exhibited each year. Below are just a few of those that have caught the attention of the older hands and spurred on the new enthusiasts. My thanks go to Neil Tyers, currently the Secretary of the Midland and West Section of the N.A.P.S. and one of today's most successful growers, for his advice and assistance.

Bob Taylor of Shipley has produced a number of new Green Edges, which have stood up well to the older varieties and have the advantage of youthful vigour. 'Clipper' is the most widely distributed, a paler shade of green than many but contrasting well with the black body and fine, white paste. Should you come across a Green Edge with a cricketing echo to its name ('Hutton' or 'Hambledon', for example), you will know its provenance.

More Greens are on the way from Chris Gill of Halifax who is acknowledged as one of the most accomplished growers of Show Auriculas for many years. Two that have already appeared on the show bench are 'Snydal' and 'Old Sage'. The edge of a Green Edge usually has a shiny surface. In the case of 'Old Sage', this is almost matt, hence the name; but it is a lovely shade of lighter green. 'Snydal', even newer, is beautifully formed and brightly coloured with a neat, smooth, golden tube. Amongst the Grey Edges, Chris has given us 'Seapeep', which is rapidly making its presence felt across the land. It is a strong, refined mid-grey of classic proportions with a remarkable zest for life. This plant is fast becoming a classic. Put it on the shopping list.

The Selfs have not been lacking amongst the newcomers. Steve Popple has come up with even more new Blues such as 'El Zoco', while Brian Coop has given us a fascinating example of orange with 'Doug Lochhead'. Forty years ago, this would have been declared a pipedream. Today it is an elegant delight.

Amongst the Alpines, Ken Bowser recently introduced the bright, dark brown to orange-yellow shaded 'Gerry Thompson', named in honour of a true eccentric, whom I once saw ride a vintage tricycle through the centre of Bradford. This plant is limited in its circulation at the moment but is highly regarded by the growers. A variety that is fast becoming a modern standard is Ed Pickin's 'Dragon's Hoard'. This is again dark brown to orange to peach, but it has a refinement belying its vigour and its willingness to produce a large truss of bloom that would have spellbound the growers of a century ago. Ed has also given us a controversial plant in the gold-centred 'Ring of Fire'. Here the shading is too abrupt for the plant to be pitted against the accepted Alpines, but may be exhibited as a Fancy. It is controversially referred to as a Laced Alpine with a dark, almost black inner zone that runs suddenly into a glowing orange-yellow ring at the edge. Both stand out strongly against the gold of the centre. Not a plant for the traditionalist, but what an eye-catcher!

Henry Pugh has continued to spread before us a range of Fancy Auriculas that appeal to the eye of all but the most conservative. They range from the almost Edged types through Picotees to Shaded Selfs of a plethora of colours. If you spot a name that would fit somewhere on a London Transport map or a Monopoly board, you can be pretty certain that it is one of Henry's multitude. Just look at the show results. He has also come up with some more conventional varieties such as the Yellow Self, 'Piccadilly', and the Red, 'Bank Error'.

One of the progenitors of the Picotees amongst Henry's range, is Randall Dee's 'Innominata'. This is reputed to be a cross between two European primulas, which throws up a good truss of blooms on a stout scape. It carries a disc of farina at the centre surrounded by a dark purple zone with a fine wire edge of white meal all round the periphery. On its first appearance, none of the current crop of growers had ever seen anything like this one and it is being used to breed more of a similar type.

John Powell has taken over the baton for Striped Auriculas from Derek Parsons. His new line of Stripes with the 'Regency' prefix show smooth edges, great refinement and a wide range of colours.

Border Auriculas have become more popular with breeders eschewing plants that are too close to the established genres. One of the most striking is 'Reddown Rainman' from Cheryl Hebdon of Bath. This very dark red puts up strong stems in good numbers, making for the type of floriferous plant that would decorate any garden border.

The Doubles continue to grow in popularity with the breeders. Lesley Roberts showed us 'Brickmakers', a striking red from Hazel Wood. It is certainly one to look out for. Pat Salt has a beautiful, pale, creamy white of excellent form, 'Poacher's Starlight', appropriate for any product of Lincolnshire. Pat's husband, Derek, has brought together his lines of striped and green Doubles in one amazing creation with green petals (the green being pigment and not foliage) enhanced by fine white lines of farina radiating out from the centre; this has the fitting name of 'Jack Frost'. While not carrying as many petals as some, it is a delight to the eye.

The beautiful bloom of 'Daisy Wood' (Photograph by Terry Mitchell)

Perhaps the last word should be kept for another Double, again from Hazel Wood and named for her mother-in-law. On its first showing, it was acclaimed as one of the most beautiful Auriculas seen in recent years. Since then, 'Daisy Wood' has won a multitude of awards. Not an easy plant to propagate, it is not readily obtainable but the pips with their texture of crystalline, greenish-white silk, sprinkled with tiny glints, each recalling a precisely formed camellia, make up a serene head of bloom which will remain with the spectator long after the flowers have faded.

CONTACTS AND SUPPLIERS

CONTACTS

The National Auricula and Primula Society is divided into three sections with a small sub-branch in Kent and the neighbouring areas. The Honorary Secretaries for each section change periodically. At the moment they are:

Midland and West Section

Neil Tyers
6 St. David's Crescent
Coalville,
Leics. LE67 4SS
www.auriculaandprimula.org.uk

Northern Section

R. Taylor
27 Temple Rhydding Drive, Baildon, Shipley,
W. Yorks. BD17 5PX
www.auriculas.org.uk

Southern Section

Lawrence Wigley
67 Warnham Court Road, Carshalton
Beeches, Surrey SM5 3ND
www.southernauriculaprimula.org

Kent Group

Colin Humphrey
32 Georgian Way, Wigmore, Rainham,
Gillingham, Kent ME8 0QZ
www.napskentgroup.org

The Scottish Auricula and Primula Society

Alison Goldie
3 Balfour Cottages, Menmuir, by Brechin,
Angus DD9 7RN
www.thescottishauriculaandprimulasociety.com

SUPPLIERS

The number of suppliers varies from time to time. Any good web search engine should find some. If you are unable to find any links, you may care to try:

Angusplants

www.angusplants.co.uk

Ashwood Nurseries

Greensforge, Kingswinford,
W. Midlands DY6 0AE
www.ashwood-nurseries.co.uk

Drointon Nurseries

Plaster Pitts, Norton Conyers, Ripon,
N. Yorks. HG4 5EF
www.auricula-plants.co.uk

Field House Nurseries

Leake House, Gotham,
Notts. NG11 0JN
List available via the Midland and
West Section web site.

Pop's Plants

Pop's Cottage, Barford Lanc, Downton,
Salisbury, Wilts. SP5 3PZ
www.popsplants.co.uk

FURTHER READING

Year Books published by all three Sections of the National Auricula and
Primula Society

Auriculas – Gwen Baker and Peter Ward (Batsford 1995)

Auriculas for Everyone – Mary Robinson (Guild of Mastercraftsmen
Publications 2000)

The Auricula – Rowland Biffen (Garden Book Club 1949)

Die Aurikel – Brigitte Wachsmuth and Marion Nickig (Ellert und Richter
Verlag) [reasonable knowledge of German needed but wonderful
illustrations may justify the purchase regardless]

Florists' Flowers and Societies – Ruth Duthie (Shire Garden History 1998)

Primulas Old and New – Jack Wemyss-Cooke (David and Charles 1986)

All of the guides published by the National Auricula and Primula Society
(Midlands and West) are written by experts with new growers in mind but
are also read by very experienced enthusiasts

RHS booklets on Primroses and Auriculas, though their slight nature
precludes many details

INDEX

Page numbers in **bold** type refer to illustrations and captions

T

J. Beswick   G. Thor
14   15

Photograph of Members taken by Joe Edwards, at the Botanical Gardens, Old Trafford, Manchester, on Saturday. 26th April, 1896. (See 30 and 3.)

2
Frank Simonite   Richard Gorton   T. La
3
Wm. Dymock   John Beswick